A NOSEGAY

CONTENTS

INTRODUCTION

They haven't got no noses,
The fallen sons of Eve;
Even the smell of roses
Is not what they supposes;
But more than mind discloses
And more than men believe.

G.K. Chesterton,
The Song of Quoodle

I plead guilty to Chesterton's charge. Mine is a mediocre specimen of a post-lapsarian nose. As a fallen daughter of Eve – or, more accurately, a fallen granddaughter of a sharp-nosed chimpanzee – I am conscious of smell only a few times each day. I put on perfume in the morning, but because I use the same concoction every day and therefore suffer from what the perfumers call "nasal fatigue", I apply far more than I should, and end up fatiguing the noses of my fellow passengers on the train en route to work. Occasionally, I sniff the milk to see if it's off, but more often I just glance at the sell-by date. Visual clues are more reliable than olfactory ones for a two-legged fallen human. On buses or in underground trains, forced during rush hour into sardine-like proximity with a smelly person, I might – with due subtlety – shade my nose from the worst of his (or her) emissions. But for most of the day, it is unusual for me to notice any particular smells. I do eat food, of course, but with the illusory impression that I am tasting rather than smelling the myriad different flavours that make up even an ordinary meal.

I am not alone in my olfactory bubble. We have been turning up our noses at smell for centuries. Some two thousand years after Aristotle blithely labelled smell the most undistinguished of all our senses, Immanuel Kant denigrated it as the "least rewarding and the most easily dispensable" of the five. He viewed it as more likely to bring disgust than pleasure, and as, at best, a "negative condition" of our well-being. In other words, we can use smell to avoid noxious air and rotting food. Kant perhaps would have been grateful for sell-by dates and the chance to abandon such an inferior sense altogether. Predictably, it was left to the French to champion the sensual in a rationalist age. In 1754 Jean-Jacques Rousseau extolled smell as "the sense of imagination" and his contemporary Jean-François Saint-Lambert lauded the nose for giving us "the most immediate sensations" and "a more immediate pleasure, more independent of the mind" than the eye. A century later, French olfactory enthusiasm had seeped across the border into Germany, where in 1888 *enfant terrible* Frederick Nietzsche somewhat bewilderingly announced: "All my genius is in my nostrils."

Should we, like Nietzsche, be guided by our nostrils? Whether or not they will kindle our imaginative genius, they might at least aid our physical survival. We no longer need to smell prey or predators, but there is evidence to suggest that we can use our sense of smell to recognise and avoid illness. In 1897 Gould and Pyle suggested in their medical handbook that lunatics could be identified by their smell: "Fèvre says the odor of the sweat of lunatics resembles that of yellow deer or mice... Burrows declares that in the absence of further evidence he would not hesitate to pronounce a person insane if he could perceive certain odors." A century of medical science later, some doctors still claim to be guided by the nose. Psychiatrists talk about an odour specific to schizophrenia and Dr Lewis Goldfrank recently told the National Geographic that he uses his nose to make snap decisions in the emergency ward. Apparently the breath of a diabetic in coma smells sweet, and a whiff of garlic can signfy arsenic poisoning. Specially trained dogs seem able to detect some cancers by examining the odours of a patient's breath (p. 104) and it is not beyond the realm of possibility that canine medical staff will pace the corridors of our future hospitals.

Perhaps our first step in raising ourselves from our fallen state should be simply to notice the ordinary smells that surround us. The people most vociferous in their praise of smell tend to be anosmics – people who have lost their olfactory powers altogether. In the words of one anosmic man I spoke to: "More than twenty four years later I deeply miss certain scents and smells. Life is lived rather like the boy in the bubble who suffered from total allergy. Many people have observed how 'fortunate' I am to be unaware of the many unpleasant smells in our world; many people are ignorant fools. Without the constant reinforcement one forgets ... the smell of flowers, of fresh cut grass, of a lover, of one's children, a glass of wine, a bonfire, the sea, the countryside after rain. The list is endless and timeless." It is important to bear in mind that losing one's sense of smell involves losing almost all of one's sense of taste. We are able actually to taste only six flavours: sweet, sour, salt, bitter, umani (richness) and astringent, and all tastes are a combination of these. The sense of taste is comprised of only one million receptor cells, as compared with around forty million for smell, and the possible palette of smells is literally infinite. When we think we are tasting, we are usually smelling. This knowledge may help us appreciate the privations of the anosmic.

The literary champion of smell, more than Marcel Proust or Patrick Süskind, is Helen Keller. Growing up blind and deaf, Keller was forced to rely on her sense of smell for basic information about her surroundings, and found in the process that it became a frequent source of intense pleasure. She lamented the fact that smell "does not hold the high position it deserves among its sisters", adding, "I doubt if there is any sensation arising from sight more delightful than the odors which filter through sun-warmed, wind-tossed branches, or the tide of scents which swells, subsides, rises again wave on wave, filling the wide world with invisible sweetness." The quotations from Keller in the course of this book illustrate the potential richness of the olfactory world, even for the biologically modern human. She went so far as to claim that she could judge character simply by sniffing, and modern scientific studies have backed her up. Generally, partners who like the smell of each other's pheromones are more likely to get married than partners who don't. Perhaps with training we could teach ourselves to sniff out future irascible wives and slobbish husbands.

Reading Helen Keller, we can perhaps learn something of what life was like for our primate ancestors. In primitive animals the bulk of the brain was formed by the limbic lobe, which is still the locus for immediate sensations such as smell. Millennia of development in the brain have led to the reduction of the limbic lobe, which has become covered with cerebral cortex. Humankind, even in its most primitive form, had a brain very similar to ours now, yet we have a much weaker sense of smell than our cave-dwelling ancestors. Indeed, congenital anosmia is on the increase, so the whole human race may be heading for an anosmic future. Characteristically, Freud suggests that ancient psycho-sexual anxieties are behind this decline in our nasal capabilities. For him, it all began when man raised himself from the ground to walk on two feet, flashing his genitals to all and sundry. The shame of this sudden exposure, the theory goes, triggered a species-wide repression of the sense of smell. Humans found genitals less embarrassing when they were seen but not smelt. This meant that men were no longer able to smell menstruation or ovulation. Smell became less important in creating sexual excitement, and humans began to be turned on more by the look of each other's bodies than the odour. As evidence for this view of smell as a forbidden, repressed sensation, Freud cites the fact that his hysterical patients often had extremely sensitive noses (see the case history of Lucy R., quoted on p. 214).

More recently, Michael Stoddart has rethought Freud's theory in more anthropological terms. Like Freud, he believes that when humans became bi-pedal, it ceased to be desirable for women to advertise menstruation and ovulation through smell signals. Stoddart, however, does not attribute this to a new sense of shame, but to the increased importance of the pair bond. Upright, earth-bound offspring – toddlers – needed more looking after than their more chimp-like predecessors. It was therefore no longer socially advantageous for the father to be tempted away from the family unit by the irresistible smells of his friends' ovulating wives. The problem here, as Stoddart himself admits, is that evolution tends to fulfill the needs of the individual rather than of the community. It still seems useful for the individual male to be attracted to other women at reproductively auspicious times, just as it seems useful for his pair-bonded partner to have the attention – and seed – of other virile men. Colourful as they are, both Freud's and Stoddart's theories have a somewhat tenuous logic. The most persuasive explanation of the decline in our nasal powers remains the most obvious: in a society where food is packaged and predators tend to attack from afar with bombs, smell has become relatively unimportant.

Despite the general decline in the human sense of smell, there are still many people in the world for whom smells are a continual source both of information and of pleasure. These people tend not to live in the West. In the developing world, where food comes straight from the forest rather than the supermarket, and is not wrapped in plastic and stamped with a sell-by date, people rely on their noses to stay alive. Unsurprisingly, some of these cultures privilege smell as a mystical, life-giving sense. For the Ongee, who live in the Andaman Islands in the South Pacific, smell provides the vital force in the universe. Ongee people sign "me" by pointing to their noses and greet each other with the question "How is your nose?" A reverence for smell can persist even in cultures where it is not necessary for survival. In both China and Japan, it still forms the basis for important rituals such as the tea ceremony (see p. 93), and in Japan people play a game called Kodo, which involves identifying specific scents. Some ordinary people can identify two-and-a-half thousand different smells.

Our lamentable sense of smell in the West seems to stem from laziness as well as evolution. The example of Helen Keller suggests that we could smell well if we really needed to. One contemporary daughter of Eve whose nasal powers seem to have bucked the evolutionary trend is Evelyn Lauder, daughter-in-law of Estée Lauder and chief nose for the Lauder perfume industry. While pregnant with her second child, she awoke one morning to discover that her sense of smell had become peculiarly acute. Happily, this new-found sensitivity has endured beyond pregnancy, and, like Helen Keller (but unlike Kant) Lauder finds that her nose brings her more pleasure than pain. When I spoke to her she had just been to Central Park in New York to "see" the spring flowers. But for her the experience was more about smelling than seeing: "the whole air was perfumed with all the lilac bushes which were in bloom and my delight in going up there was to smell the exquisite aromas of all the various flowers." She is saddened by how little we notice smell in the West, and points out that our children tend to be far more nasally driven than we are. Lauder even temporarily doffs her perfume magnate hat to caution nursing mothers against wearing perfume or perfumed creams, as they can hamper the natural bonding process and even prevent the baby from recognising the mother.

I find this rather unnerving. If perfume inhibits babies' natural reactions to other people's smells, surely adults are to some extent also affected – particularly adults with a sense of smell as precarious as ours. It is strange that, in a culture so desensitised to smell, most women still wear perfume almost every day and about fifty new fragrances are produced each year. Two millennia ago, Pliny made the same observation, complaining about the time and money wasted on perfume given that the wearer doesn't even derive much pleasure from it him or herself (p. 76). Several men I've spoken to in the course of my research have bemoaned the way women cover up their natural smells of sweat and pheromones. On page 123 an American man commits these feelings eloquently to paper, lamenting his perennial failure to find a vagina that really smells of vagina. He longs to bottle what he sees as the true scent of a woman.

In seeking to cover up our own pheromones and sexual secretions, we have traditionally turned to the pheromones of animals. Until recently, the majority of perfumers used musk and civet in their concoctions. Musk is produced in small quantities by young Himalayan musk deer during the mating season; the animal has to be killed in order to remove the small pod in which it is contained. Civet is scraped from the anal pouches of civet cats of both sexes: a disagreeable but not necessarily fatal procedure. Over the centuries, civet and musk have been sources both of delight and danger for perfume wearers. In 1688, Petrus Castellus extolled the wonders of civet for increasing sexual appetite, and in 1897 Gould and Pyle warned of the somewhat sticky predicament of a couple who over-indulged in musk (see p. 80). Perfumers can now produce a synthetic copy of both musk and civet, and nobody in America or Europe uses actual animal secretions. Nevertheless, it seems anomalous that we go to such lengths to disguise our own pheromones, merely to replace them with the simulated pheromones of other animals.

For Evelyn Lauder it is not a question of disguising, but rather of accessorising our natural smell: "Women should have a wardrobe of fragrances, the way they have a wardrobe of clothing, the way they have a wardrobe of shoes." She is adamant that perfumes complement rather than crush natural odours, and that each person's body chemistry makes the oils project differently. For her, perfume seems to be at once an aesthetic and a sensual pleasure, much like art or music. In this she resembles Coco Chanel, whose wonderful maxims on life and perfume appear in the Smell Industry chapter. Chanel, too, had an amazing sense of smell: she coyly claims on p. 73 to be able to smell the hand that picked any flower she is given.

Lyall Watson, in his book *Jacobson's Organ and the Remarkable Nature of Smell*, points to some of the potential benefits of rescuing "our most underrated sense from obscurity." He suggests that with a little training we could smell "which way the children went, who their friends are, who last used this chair or slept in that bed, and whether they were alone, when the girl next door ovulates and is likely to be attractive to, or a threat to others, what our spouses had for lunch, and who they spent that time with, and whether or not we are going to need a lawyer." These are spectacular claims, and if Watson's imaginary sniffer existed, he would surpass Coco Chanel or Evelyn Lauder, and even Sherlock Holmes, the cohort of a more famous Watson (see p. 88). Perhaps only Helen Keller's extraordinary gifts of nasal detection hint that Watson's visions are not altogether utopian – or indeed dystopian.

For Watson, the issue is not so much the sense of smell itself, as the vomeronasal organs, commonly known as Jacobson's organs. These are small pits near the front of the nasal septum, about a centimetre and a half in from each nostril, just above the floor of the nose. They do not register ordinary odours. Instead, they respond to substances that have large molecules and no particular odour, including pheromones. It is Jacobson's organ, if trained well, that can help us "smell a rat" or "smell something fishy" or smell whether someone we've just met is more likely to be a future enemy or a future spouse.

* * *

If smell is the sense of the imagination, then writers are the best placed to translate it into words, and here I have gathered some of the best words of some of the best writers. Although not all the quotations are chosen for their literary merit, I hope that this book is of literary as well as cultural and olfactory interest. Most people, when describing a smell, will say little more than whether it is good or bad, though often in more florid or more scatological terms: "It smells like roses" or "It smells like shit". Writing about a sense as un- or indeed anti-literary as smell is surely one of the most difficult challenges a writer can undertake. One time-honoured way to write fragrantly is to use synaesthetic metaphors. We see Martial starting out on this route on p. 189 with his "smell of a silvery vineyard flowering with the first clusters of grass that a sheep has freshly cropped." Do we smell the sheep, we might ask, or are they part of a visual image that is somehow equivalent to the smell? The same might be asked of Mallarmé's "dizzying odour of loosened hair" which again evokes a feeling that approximates to that evoked by the smell, rather than describing the smell itself (p. 195).

Proust, of course, is the master of synaesthesia and extended metaphor. For him the countryside reverberates with odours so evocative that they assume human traits: "smells lazy and punctual as a village clock, roving and settled, heedless and provident" (p. 200). The scent of the hawthorn takes on the intensity of music: it has a "rhythm which disposed the flowers here and there with a youthful light-heartedness" (p. 213). More recently, Thomas Pynchon's description of breakfast in *Gravity's Rainbow* has undertones of Proust and of Martial. The "mucaceous odor of Breakfast" is "flowery, permeating, surprising, more than the color of winter sunlight" (p. 160). Like Martial, Pynchon colours the smell. Perhaps colour is one of the most effective ways of describing an odour: our reactions to both tend to be immediate and emotionally driven.

A new arrival on the synaesthetic literary scene is Luca Turin, a chemist whose chief contribution to olfactory science is his theory of how we smell. In *The Secret of Scent*, he rumbustiously dethrones the widely accepted notion that the smell of a molecule depends solely on its shape, asserting instead that the vibrations within the molecule play the crucial role. However, Turin is obviously motivated by more than just scientific curiosity in his search for the olfactory holy grail, and his perfume guide, *Parfum*, written in 1992 during a break from scientific pursuits, reads at moments as a Proustian remembrance of fragrances past. Nombre Noir, for instance, is "half-way between a rose and a violet" and "glistening with a liquid freshness that made its colours glow like a stained-glass window" (p. 90). Turin believes that his edge in turning smell into language is due to the fact that for him "smell has always had an utterly solid reality" and is astonished that others do not share this experience. For Turin, every perfume he has ever smelled has been "like a movie, sound and vision." While Proust's synaesthetic descriptions remain metaphorical, Turin seems genuinely to experience smell in several dimensions, and it is this that gives power to his writing.

Other writers strive to categorise smells, rather than to find emotional or visual analogues for them. Coleridge is being literal when he observes in his notebook that a dead dog smells like elder-flowers (p. 198). Similarly, Thomas Wolfe conveys complex smells to the reader by itemising their component parts, listing odours that may be more familiar: "He knew the good male smell of his father's sitting room, of the smooth worn leather sofa, with the gaping horsehair rent, of the blistered varnished wood upon the hearth; of the heated calf skin bindings; of the flat moist plug of Apple tobacco." (p. 201) The most famous practitioner of this kind of writing is Patrick Süskind. In his 1985 novel, *Perfume*, the smells of a baby are listed as warm stone, butter and a pancake soaked in milk, while the smell of the most beautiful girl Grenouille has ever smelt is likened to a combination of silk and pastry soaked in honey-sweet milk. Like Wolfe, Süskind provides a disparate collection of mostly familiar smells, allowing us to home in on the exact smell. Unlike Wolfe, though, he allows the synaesthetic to impinge on his smell-collage. The baby surely feels like warm stone as much as it smells like it, and the silk and the girl share a visual and tactile rather than an olfactory beauty. In reality, silk has a slightly unpleasant, fishy odour. Unfortunately, Süskind does not permit his lovingly bottled smells to be extracted as scratch-and-sniff samples, so there are no quotations from *Perfume* in this book.

From this short survey of some of the literary approaches to smell used by the writers in this book, it is clear that writers in Ancient Rome, modernist France and post-modern America are essentially tackling the same problem. And as you sniff your way across the centuries from Aristotle to the internet, you will notice how much continuity there is, not just in the writing technique but in the smells themselves. The thematic structure of the collection is intended to emphasise this continuity, juxtaposing writers who are far apart in time but close together in smell. Catullus found hairy armpits as noisome as the Americans find them in France today. The seventeenth century poet Robert Herrick found Julia's sweat as much of a turn-on as Napoleon did Josephine's two centuries later. (He famously sent word from the thick of battle that she should abstain from washing now that his return was nigh.) The American man longing to bottle the scent of vagina finds his place at the end of this trajectory of secretion-loving men.

I have avoided dwelling too long on some of the historical smells that are hardest to forget. It is clear from the chapter about death that the smell of decaying human flesh is one of the most evocative and the most remembered. Included in the historical smells chapter are descriptions of some of the worst battle-fields in history, and two particularly moving accounts of the reek of the concentration camps. Although the tone of this book is essentially light-hearted, these extracts are potent reminders of some of the worst stenches we have known, and might help us to appreciate the more pleasant aromas that surround most of us now.

In 1952 Le Gros Clark suggested that Descartes' *Cogito ergo sum* should be changed to *Olfacio ergo cogito*. Proust, perhaps, would go so far as to change it to *Olfacio ergo sum*. Either seems a good endorsement for learning to smell. I hope that this book will enrich your noses and your olfactory vocabularies. Next time you smell a pile of manure you can say that it smells like durian. Next time you smell some roses you can say – if you think you can get away with it – that they have a dizzying odour of loosened hair. We will never again be apes or know the exquisite aromas of a pre-lapsarian Paradise. This need not stop us, as Walter Hagen puts it, from smelling the flowers along the way.

Lara Feigel
September 2006

You're only here for a short visit. Don't hurry, don't worry. And be sure to smell the flowers along the way.

Walter Hagen

I have here only made a nosegay of culled flowers, and have brought nothing of my own but the thread that ties them together

Michel de Montaigne

I know every book of mine by its smell, and I have but to put my nose between the pages to be reminded of all sorts of things.

George Gissing

CHAPTER I

"A *fierce* goat lives in your armpits"

Human Scents and Stinks

HUMAN odors are as varied and capable of recognition as hands and faces. The dear odors of those I love are so definite, so unmistakable, that nothing can quite obliterate them. If many years should elapse before I saw an intimate friend again, I think I should recognise his odor instantly in the heart of Africa, as promptly as would my brother that barks.

Once, long ago, in a crowded railway station, a lady kissed me as she hurried by. I had not touched even her dress. But she left a scent with her kiss which gave me a glimpse of her. The years are many since she kissed me. Yet her odor is fresh in my memory...

Some people have a vague, unsubstantial odor that floats about, mocking every effort to identify it. It is the will-o-the-wisp of my olfactive experience. Sometimes I meet one who lacks a distinctive person-scent, and I seldom find such a one lively or entertaining. On the other hand, one who had a pungent odor often possesses great vitality, energy, and vigor of mind.

Masculine exhalations are as a rule stronger, more vivid, more widely differentiated than those of women. In the odor of young men there is something elemental, as of fire, storm, and salt sea. It pulsates with buoyancy and desire. It suggests all things strong and beautiful and joyous, and gives me a sense of physical happiness. I wonder if others observe that all infants have the same scent – pure, simple, undecipherable as their dormant personality. It is not until the age of six or seven that they begin to have perceptible individual odors. These develop and mature with their mental and bodily powers.

Helen Keller, Sense and Sensibility, 1907

IF you cut a thing up, of course it will smell. Hence, nothing raises such an infernal stink at last, as human psychology.

D.H. Lawrence, St Mawr, 1925

DON'T be surprised that no woman's willing, Rufus
To place her tender thigh under you
Even if you undermine her with sheerest silk
Or gifts of translucent gems.
A certain wicked rumour's harming you: they say
A fierce goat lives in your armpits,
Everyone's afraid. No wonder: for it's a right
Awful beast no nice girl could sleep with.
So either destroy this cruel, nasal pestilence
Or stop wondering why you're shunned.

Catullus, Poem 69,
Odorous: To Rufus, c54 BC

DIVINE am I inside and out, and I make holy whatever
I touch or am touch'd from,
The scent of these arm-pits aroma finer than prayer,
This head more than churches, bibles, and all the creeds.

Walt Whitman, Song of Myself, 1855

WHO'D ye oil of blossoms get?
　　Take it from my Julia's sweat;
Oil of lilies, and of spike,
From her moisture take the like;
Let her breathe, or let her blow,
All rich spices thence will flow.

Robert Herrick,
Upon Julia's Sweat, 1648

COMING to kiss her lips (such grace I found)
　　Me seemed I smelt a garden of sweet flowers:
That dainty odours from them threw around
For damsels fit to deck their lovers bowers.
Her lips did smell like unto Gillyflowers,
Her ruddy cheeks like unto Roses red:
Her snowy brows like budded Bellamoures,
Her lovely eyes like Pinks but newly spread.
Her goodly bosom like a Strawberry bed,
Her neck like to a bunch of Cullambynes:
Her breast like lilies, ere their leaves be shed,
Her nipples like young blossom's Jessemynes.
Such fragrant flowers do give most odourous smell,
But her sweet odour did them all excel.

Edmund Spenser,
Coming to Kiss Her Lips, 1595

MY mistress' eyes are nothing like the sun;
Coral is far more red than her lips' red;
If snow be white, why then her breasts are dun;
If hairs be wires, black wires grow on her head.
I have seen roses damask'd, red and white,
But no such roses see I in her cheeks,
And in some perfumes is there more delight
Than in the breath that from my mistress reeks.

William Shakespeare, Sonnet 130, c1600

SAY that the sense of feeling were bereft me,
And that I could not see, nor hear, nor touch,
And nothing but the very smell were left me,
Yet would my love to thee be still as much,
For from the stillitory of thy face excelling
Comes breath perfumed that breedeth love by smelling.

William Shakespeare, Venus and Adonis, 1593

"THAT is true," quoth Don Quixote; "but thinkest thou not that the tallness of her extended stature is adorned with as thousand millions of graces and endowments of the soul? But, Sancho, thou canst not deny me one thing: when thou didst thus approach her, didst thou not feel a most odoriferous smell, an aromatical fragrancy, an – I cannot tell what, so pleasing as I know not how to term it – I say such a scent as if thou wert in some curious perfumer's shop?" "That which I know," quoth Sancho, "is that I felt a little unsavoury scent, somewhat rammish and man-like, and I think the reason was because she had sweat a little doing of that exercise."

. . .

But she was scarce come to the door when Don Quixote felt her, and, arising and sitting up in his bed, in despite of his plaisters and with great grief of his ribs, he stretched forth his arms to receive his beautiful damsel, the Asturian, who, crouching and silently, went groping with her hands to find out her sweet heart, and encountered Don Quixote's arms, who presently seized very strongly upon one of her wrists, and, drawing her towards him (she daring not to speak a word), he caused her to sit upon his bed's side, and presently groped her smock, and although it was of the strongest canvas, he thought it was most subtle and fine holland. She wore on her wrists certain bracelets of glass, which he esteemed to be precious oriental pearls. Her hair which was almost as rough as a horse-tail, he held to be wires of the glisteringest gold of Arabia, whose brightness did obscure that of the sun; and her breath, which certainly smelled like to stale salt-fish reserved from over night, seemed unto him a most redolent, aromatical, and sweet smell.

Miguel de Cervantes, Don Quixote, 1605

HE stood aside, edged a little into the rain to let the throng pass. A small boy rushed out, sniffed in the damp, fresh air and turned up the collar of his coat; came three or four couples in a great hurry; came a further scattering of people whose eyes as they emerged glanced invariably, first at the wet street, then at the rain-filled air, finally at the dismal sky; last a dense, strolling mass that depressed him with its heavy odor compounded of the tobacco smell of the men and the fetid sensuousness of stale powder on women. After the thick crowd came another scattering; a stray half-dozen; a man on crutches; finally the rattling bang of folding seats inside announced that the ushers were at work.

F. Scott Fitzgerald, *This Side of Paradise*, 1920

GUESTS, like fish, begin to smell after three days.

Benjamin Franklin,
Poor Richard's Almanack, 1733-1758

A man has his distinctive personal scent which his wife, his children and his dog can recognize. A crowd has a generalized stink. The public is odourless.

W.H. Auden, *The Poet and the City*, 1962

ON Easter Monday we went up to visit the Murrys & see Hampstead Heath. Our verdict was that the crowd at close quarters is detestable; it smells; it sticks; it has neither vitality nor colour; it is a tepid mass of flesh scarcely organised into human life. How slow they walk! How passively & brutishly they lie on the grass!

Virginia Woolf, *Diary*, April 1919

THE sailor's customs are debauched; he finds supreme happiness in drunkenness; the odour of tobacco, wedded to the vapours of wine, alcohol, garlic, and the other coarse foods that he likes to eat, the perfume of his clothing often impregnated with sweat, filth, and tar make it repulsive to be near him.

Charles-Polydore Forget,
Médicine Navale, 1828

MY brother Stephen sits in the front seat, beside the partly open window. He smells of peppermint LifeSavers; underneath that is his ordinary smell, of cedarwood lead pencils and wet sand. Sometimes he throws up into paper bags, or beside the road if my father can stop the car in time... Boys don't smell the same as girls. They have a pungent, leathery, underneath smell, like old rope, like damp dogs.

Margaret Atwood, Cat's Eye, 1988

THE strong, savage odour of the two habitués of the highway made the dining room stink so much that it offended Madame de Montcornet's delicate senses and she would have been forced to leave if Mouche and Fourchon had stayed any longer.

Honoré de Balzac, Les Paysans, 1844

THAT was what we were taught – the lower classes smell...
You can have an affection for a murderer or a sodomite,
but you cannot have an affection for a man whose breath stinks
– habitually stinks, I mean... And in my childhood we were
brought up to believe that they were dirty... You watched a
great sweaty navvy walking down the road with his pick over
his shoulder; you looked at his discoloured shirt and his corduroy
trousers stiff with the dirt of a decade; you thought of those nests
and layers of greasy rags below, and, under all, the unwashed body,
brown all over (that was how I used to imagine it), with its strong,
bacon-like reek... The smell of their sweat, the very texture of
their skins, were mysteriously different from yours.

George Orwell, The Road to Wigan Pier, 1937

IN the West we are divided from our fellows by our sense of
smell. The working man is our master, inclined to rule us with
an iron hand, but it cannot be denied that he stinks: none can
wonder at it, for a bath in the dawn when you have to hurry to
your work before the factory bell rings is no pleasant thing, nor
does heavy labour tend to sweetness; and you do not change your
linen more than you can help when the week's washing must be
done by a sharp-tongued wife. I do not blame the working man
because he stinks, but stink he does. It makes social intercourse
difficult to persons of sensitive nostril. The matutinal tub divides
the classes more effectually than birth, wealth, or education.

W. Somerset Maugham, On a Chinese Screen, 1955

THE sermon began. The room was stuffy and smelly. The mixture of body odors and cooking was nauseating. I remember thinking: How can these people share this facility? They must be repulsed by each other. They had strange habits and dispositions. They were a group of dirty, dishonoured, weird people to me. When it was over I ran to my car, went home and took a shower. I felt extremely dirty. Through the day I would get flashes of that disgusting smell.

Peter Marin and Anna Quindlen,
Helping and Hating the Homeless,
San Francisco Chronicle, 1987

I would have every man so much like a wild antelope, so much a part and parcel of nature, that his very person should thus sweetly advertise our senses of his presence, and remind us of those parts of nature which he most haunts. I feel no disposition to be satirical, when the trapper's coat emits the odor of musquash even; it is a sweeter scent to me than that which commonly exhales from the merchant's or the scholar's garments. When I go into their wardrobes and handle their vestments, I am reminded of no grassy plains and flowery meads ... but of dusty merchants' exchanges and libraries rather.

Henry David Thoreau, Walking, 1862

STREPHON, who found the Room was void,
And Betty otherwise employed;
Stole in, and took a strict Survey,
Of all the Litter as it lay ...

Why Strephon will you tell the rest?
And must you needs describe the Chest?
That careless Wench! no Creature warn her
To move it out from yonder Corner;
But leave it standing full in Sight
For you to exercise your Spite.
In vain, the Workman shewed his Wit
With Rings and Hinges counterfeit
To make it seem in this Disguise,
A Cabinet to vulgar Eyes;
For Strephon ventured to look in,
Resolved to go through thick and thin;
He lifts the Lid, there needs no more,
He smelt it all the Time before.

As from within Pandora's Box,
When Epimetheus oped the Locks,
A sudden universal Crew
Of humane Evils upwards flew;
He still was comforted to find
That Hope at last remained behind;

So Strephon lifting up the Lid,
To view what in the Chest was hid.
The Vapours flew from out the Vent,
But Strephon cautious never meant
The Bottom of the Pan to grope,
And fowl his Hands in Search of Hope.

O never may such vile Machine
Be once in Celia's Chamber seen!
O may she better learn to keep
"Those Secrets of the hoary deep!"

Jonathan Swift, Her Lady's Dressing Room, 1732

EVERY man's ordure well
To his own sense doth smell

Roman Proverb,
Terence, Andria, c. 195 BC

EVERY man likes the smell of his own farts.

Icelandic Proverb

WHERE there is a stink of shit there is a smell of being.

Antonin Artaud,
The Pursuit of Fecality, 1947

BUT, however, let her be one of the supremest dignity of countenance, let the power of Venus radiate from her whole body, the truth is there are others, the truth is we have lived so far without this one; the truth is she does the same things as the ugly woman does, and we know it, fumigating herself the poor wretch with rank odours while her maidservants give her a wide berth and giggle behind her back. But the lover shut out, weeping, often covers the threshold with flowers and wreaths, anoints the proud doorposts with oil of marjoram, presses his love-sick kisses upon the door; but if he is let in, once he gets but one whiff as he comes, he would seek some decent excuse for taking his leave; there would be an end of the complaint so oft rehearsed, so deeply felt, and he would condemn himself on the spot of folly, now he sees that he had attributed to her more than it is right to concede to a mortal.

Lucretius, De Rerum Natura, c60 BC

WHAT have we here? a man or a fish? dead or alive? A fish, he smells like a fish; a very ancient and fish-like smell; a kind of not-of-the-newest Poor-John. A strange fish! Were I in England now (as once I was) and had but this fish painted, not a holiday fool there but would give a piece of silver. There would this monster make a man; any strange beast there makes a man. When they will not give a doit to relieve a lame beggar, they will lay out ten to see a dead Indian. Legg'd like a man; and his fins like arms! Warm, o' my troth! I do now let loose my opinion, hold it no longer: this is no fish, but an islander, that hath lately suffer'd by a thunderbolt.

William Shakespeare, The Tempest, 1611

* * *

FRIAR John, at the approach of Panurge, was entertained with a kind of smell that was not like that of gunpowder, nor altogether so sweet as musk; which made him turn Panurge about, and then he saw that his shirt was dismally bepawed and berayed with fresh sir-reverence. The retentive faculty of the nerve which restrains the muscle called sphincter ('tis the arse-hole, an' it please you) was relaxated by the violence of the fear which he had been in during his fantastic visions. Add to this the thundering noise of the shooting, which seems more dreadful between decks than above. Nor ought you to wonder at such a mishap; for one of the symptoms and accidents of fear is, that it often opens the wicket of the cupboard wherein second-hand meat is kept for a time.

François Rabelais, Pantagruel, 1532

"**D**ICK married Nicole for her money," she said. "That was his weakness – you hinted as much yourself one night."

"You're being malicious."

"I shouldn't have said that," she retracted. "We must all live together like birds, as you say. But it's difficult when Nicole acts as – when Nicole pulls herself back a little, as if she were holding her breath – as if I SMELT bad!"

Kaethe had touched a material truth. She did most of her work herself, and, frugal, she bought few clothes. An American shopgirl, laundering two changes of underwear every night, would have noticed a hint of yesterday's reawakened sweat about Kaethe's person, less a smell than an ammoniacal reminder of the eternity of toil and decay. To Franz this was as natural as the thick dark scent of Kaethe's hair, and he would have missed it equally; but to Nicole, born hating the smell of a nurse's fingers dressing her, it was an offence only to be endured.

F. Scott Fitzgerald, Tender is the Night, 1934

DOROTHY knocked at the Pithers' badly fitting door, from beneath which a melancholy smell of boiled cabbage and dish-water was oozing. From long experience she knew and could taste in advance the individual smell of every cottage on her rounds. Some of their smells were peculiar in the extreme. For instance, there was the salty, feral smell that haunted the cottage of old Mr Tombs, an aged retired bookseller who lay in bed all day in a darkened room, with his long, dusty nose and pebble spectacles protruding from what appeared to be a fur rug of vast size and richness. But if you put your hand on the fur rug it disintegrated, burst and fled in all directions. It was composed entirely of cats – twenty- four cats, to be exact. Mr Tombs "found they kept him warm", he used to explain. In nearly all the cottages there was a basic smell of old overcoats and dish-water upon which the other, individual smells were superimposed; the cesspool smell, the cabbage smell, the smell of children, the strong, bacon-like reek of corduroys impregnated with the sweat of a decade.

George Orwell,
A Clergyman's Daughter, 1935

THE shadows of gloomy events that haunted the else lonely and desolate apartments; the heavy, breathless scent which death had left in more than one of the bedchambers, ever since his visits of long ago – these were less powerful than the purifying influence scattered throughout the atmosphere of the household by the presence of one youthful, fresh, and thoroughly wholesome heart. There was no morbidness in Phoebe; if there had been, the old Pyncheon House was the very locality to ripen it into incurable disease... Whatever was morbid in his mind and experience she ignored; and thereby kept their intercourse healthy, by the incautious, but, as it were, heaven-directed freedom of her whole conduct. The sick in mind, and, perhaps, in body, are rendered more darkly and hopelessly so by the manifold reflection of their disease, mirrored back from all quarters in the deportment of those about them; they are compelled to inhale the poison of their own breath, in infinite repetition. But Phoebe afforded her poor patient a supply of purer air. She impregnated it, too, not with a wild-flower scent – for wildness was no trait of hers – but with the perfume of garden-roses, pinks, and other blossoms of much sweetness, which nature and man have consented together in making grow from summer to summer, and from century to century. Such a flower was Phoebe in her relation with Clifford, and such the delight that he inhaled from her.

Nathaniel Hawthorne,
The House of the Seven Gables, 1851

AND his father Isaac said unto him, Come near now, and kiss me, my son.

And he came near, and kissed him: and he smelled the smell of his raiment, and blessed him, and said, See, the smell of my son is as the smell of a field which the Lord hath blessed.

Genesis, King James Version of the Bible, 1611

I began last week to permit my wife to sit at dinner with me, at the farthest end of a long table; and to answer (but with the utmost brevity) the few questions I asked her. Yet, the smell of a Yahoo continuing very offensive, I always keep my nose well stopped with rue, lavender, or tobacco leaves.

Jonathan Swift, Gulliver's Travels, 1726

THOU art asleep, and the smell of that forbidden fruit
    Ascends to the azure skies,
Ascends along with thy foul breath,
Till it overpowers heaven with stench;
Stench of pride, stench of lust, stench of greed.
All these stink like onions when a man speaks.
Though thou swearest, saying, "When have I eaten?
Have I not abstained from onions and garlic?"
The very breath of that oath tells tales,
As it strikes the nostrils of them that sit with thee.

Rumi, The Masnavi I Ma'navi, c1250

IS suffering so very serious? I have come to doubt it... It's extremely painful. I agree that it's hardly bearable. But I very much fear that this sort of pain deserves no consideration at all. It's no more worthy of respect than old age or illness, for both of which I'm acquiring a great repulsion: both of them are anxious to get me in their clutches before long, and I'm holding my nose in advance. The lovesick, the betrayed and the jealous all smell alike.

Colette, The South of France, 1925

WHEN we have ceased to love the stench of the human animal, either in others or in ourselves, then are we condemned to misery, and clear thinking can begin.

Cyril Connolly, The Unquiet Grave, 1944

HE scrambled up the mighty bean.
Up up he went without a stop,
But just as he was near the top,
A ghastly frightening thing occurred –
Not far above his head he heard
A big deep voice, a rumbling thing
That made the very heavens ring,
It shouted loud, "FE FI FO FUM
"I SMELL THE BLOOD OF
AN ENGLISHMAN!"
Jack was frightened, Jack was quick,
And down he climbed in half a tick.
"Oh mum!" he gasped. "Believe you me
"There's something nasty up our tree!
"I saw him, mum! My gizzard froze!
"A Giant with a clever nose!"
"A clever nose!" his mother hissed.
"You must be going round the twist!"
"He smelled me out, I swear it, mum!
"He said he smelled an Englishman!"
The mother said, "And well he might!
"I've told you every single night
"To take a bath because you smell,
"But would you do it? Would you hell!
"You even make your mother shrink
"Because of your unholy stink!"
Jack answered, "Well, if you're so clean
"Why don't you climb the crazy bean."
The mother cried, "By gad, I will!
"There's life within the old dog still!"
She hitched her skirts above her knee
And disappeared right up the tree.
Now would the Giant smell his mum?
Jack listened for the fee-fo-fum.
He gazed aloft. He wondered when
The dreaded words would come…

And then…
From somewhere high above the ground
There came a frightful crunching sound.
He heard the giant mutter twice,
"By gosh, that tasted very nice."…
"By Christopher!" Jack cried. "By gum!
"The Giant's eaten up my mum!
"He smelled her out! She's in his belly!
"I had a hunch that she was smelly."
Jack stood there gazing longingly
Upon the huge and golden tree.
He muttered softly, "Golly-gosh,
"I guess I'll have to take a wash
"If I am going to climb this tree
"Without the Giant smelling me.
"In fact, a bath's my only hope…'
He rushed indoors and grabbed the soap
He scrubbed his body everywhere.
He even washed and rinsed his hair.
He did his teeth, he blew his nose
And went out smelling like a rose.
Once more he climbed the mighty bean.
The Giant sat there, gross, obscene,
Muttering through his vicious teeth
(While Jack sat tensely just beneath)
Muttering loud, "FEE FI FO FUM,
"RIGHT NOW I CAN'T SMELL ANYONE."
Jack waited till the Giant slept,
Then out along the boughs he crept
And gathered so much gold, I swear
He was an instant millionaire.
"A bath," he said, "does seem to pay.
"I'm going to have one every day."

Roald Dahl, Jack and the Beanstalk, 1982

WHY is the smell of the breath heavier and more unpleasant in the deformed and stooping?

Why is the armpit the most unpleasant smelling region? Is it because less air reaches it?

Why does urine become more evil-smelling the longer it remains in the body, while dung becomes less so?

Aristotle, Problems Connected With
Unpleasant Smells, Problems, c340BC

I am most particular about my bed; it is the sanctuary of life. We entrust our almost naked and fatigued bodies to it so that they may be reanimated by reposing between soft sheets and feathers...

I cannot lift up the sheets of a hotel bed without a shudder of disgust. Who has occupied it the night before? Perhaps dirty, revolting people have slept in it. I begin, then, to think of all the horrible people with whom one rubs shoulders every day, people with suspicious-looking skin which makes one think of the feet and all the rest! I call to mind those who carry about with them the sickening smell of garlic or of humanity. I think of those who are deformed and unhealthy, of the perspiration emanating from the sick, of everything that is ugly and filthy in man. And all this, perhaps, in the bed in which I am about to sleep! The mere idea of it makes me feel ill as I get into it.

Guy de Maupassant,
The Rondoli Sisters, 1884

A S for the sense of smell, do not be so vain as to surround yourselves with amber perfumes and other sweet-smelling compounds or to use toilet water, all of which have little to recommend them, even to the laity. Rather, habituate yourselves to tolerating without disgust the unpleasant smells that so often emanate from the sick, like those saints who laboured with joy in the vilest sick wards as if they were in the midst of a garden filled with the most delicious flowers.

Saint Alphonse Marie de Liguori,
The True Spouse of Jesus Christ, 1761

T HE maids of honour often invited Glumdalclitch to their apartments, and desired she would bring me along with her, on purpose to have the pleasure of seeing and touching me. They would often strip me naked from top to toe, and lay me at full length in their bosoms; wherewith I was much disgusted because, to say the truth, a very offensive smell came from their skins; which I do not mention, or intend, to the disadvantage of those excellent ladies, for whom I have all manner of respect; but I conceive that my sense was more acute in proportion to my littleness, and that those illustrious persons were no more disagreeable to their lovers, or to each other, than people of the same quality are with us in England. And, after all, I found their natural smell was much more supportable, than when they used perfumes, under which I immediately swooned away. I cannot forget, that an intimate friend of mine in Lilliput, took the freedom in a warm day, when I had used a good deal of exercise, to complain of a strong smell about me, although I am as little faulty that way, as most of my sex: but I suppose his faculty of smelling was as nice with regard to me, as mine was to that of this people. Upon this point, I cannot forbear doing justice to the queen my mistress, and Glumdalclitch my nurse, whose persons were as sweet as those of any lady in England.

Jonathan Swift, Gulliver's Travels, 1726

BRECHT had extremely bad teeth, which he rarely brushed, and he smoked very cheap and terrible-smelling cigars, whose stench, combined with body odor (Brecht rarely bathed) and a malodorous foot fungus, rendered Brecht a party of one in the making. (Elsa Lanchester, Charles Laughton's wife, claimed that her house smelled of cigar smoke and other odors for days after Brecht had been there.)

Kevin Starr, The Dream Endures:
California Enters the 1940s, 2002

"YEH! Mr William: Why you no smelling?"

"What did you say, Balvinder?"

"Why you no smelling?"

"That's not very polite."

"Mr William. Please answer. Why you not smelling?"

"Well, if you must know, I had a bath this morning. And I always make a point of applying a little under-arm deodorant."

"No, no, Mr William. Maybe you are uncomfortable in this here hot weather. Normally you smell a lot."

"Did you just say I normally smell a lot?"

"Oh yes, Mr William," said Balvinder, shaking his head emphatically. "But these days your face is very sad."

Realising at last what he had been getting at, my expression changed to a broad grin.

"That's better," said Mr Singh. "Now at last you are smiling."

William Dalrymple, City of Djinns, 1994

WE could both wish that one's first impression of K.M. [Katherine Mansfield] was not that she stinks like a – well civet cat that had taken to street walking.

Virginia Woolf, Diary, 1917

IT has been reported of some, as of Alexander the Great, that their sweat exhaled an odoriferous smell, occasioned by some rare and extraordinary constitution, of which Plutarch and others have been inquisitive into the cause. But the ordinary constitution of human bodies is quite otherwise, and their best and chiefest excellency is to be exempt from smell. Nay, the sweetness even of the purest breath has nothing in it of greater perfection than to be without any offensive smell, like those of healthful children, which made Plautus say of a woman:

> "Mulier tum bene olet, ubi nihil olet."

> ["She smells sweetest, who smells not at all."
> –Plautus, Mostel, i. 3, 116.]

And such as make use of fine exotic perfumes are with good reason to be suspected of some natural imperfection which they endeavour by these odours to conceal. To smell, though well, is to stink:

> "Rides nos, Coracine, nil olentes
> Malo, quam bene olere, nil olere."

> ["You laugh at us, Coracinus, because we are not scented; I
> would rather than smell well, not smell at all."
> –Martial, vi. 55, 4.]

Michel de Montaigne, Of Smells, 1572-1580

STREPHON who heard the foaming rill
As from a mossy cliff distil;
Cried out, "Ye gods, what sound is this?
Can Chloe, heavenly Chloe piss?"
But, when he smelt a noisesome steam
Which oft attends that luke-warm stream;
(Salerno both together joins
As sovereign medicines for the loins)
And, though contrived, we may suppose
To slip his ears, yet struck his nose:
He found her, while the scent increased,
As mortal as himself at least.

Jonathan Swift, Strephon and Chloe, 1731

THE first, then, and highest purity is that which is in the soul... Now we ought to work at something like this in the body also, as far as we can. It was impossible for the defluxions of the nose not to run when man has such a mixture in his body. For this reason, nature has made hands and the nostrils themselves as channels for carrying off the humours. If, then, a man sucks up the defluxions, I say that he is not doing the act of a man. It was impossible for a man's feet not to be made muddy and not be soiled at all when he passes through dirty places. For this reason, nature has made water and hands... It was impossible that from the sweat and the pressing of the clothes there should not remain some impurity about the body which requires to be cleaned away. For this reason water, oil, hands, towels, scrapers, nitre, sometimes all other kinds of means are necessary for cleaning the body... "Why?" he asks. I will tell you again; in the first place, that you may do the acts of a man; then, that you may not be disagreeable to those with whom you associate. You do something of this kind even in this matter, and you do not perceive it: you think that you deserve to stink. Let it be so: deserve to stink. Do you think that also those who sit by you, those who recline at table with you, that those who kiss you deserve the same? Either go into a desert, where you deserve to go, or live by yourself, and smell yourself. For it is just that you alone should enjoy your own impurity. But when you are in a city, to behave so inconsiderately and foolishly, to what character do you think that it belongs? If nature had entrusted to you a horse, would you have overlooked and neglected him? And now think that you have been entrusted with your own body as with a horse; wash it, wipe it, take care that no man turns away from it, that no one gets out of the way for it. But who does not get out of the way of a dirty man, of a stinking man, of a man whose skin is foul, more than he does out of the way of a man who is daubed with muck? That smell is from without, it is put upon him; but the other smell is from want of care, from within, and in a manner from a body in putrefaction.

"But Socrates washed himself seldom." Yes, but his body was clean and fair: and it was so agreeable and sweet that the most beautiful and the most noble loved him, and desired to sit by him rather than by the side of those who had the handsomest forms. It was in his power neither to use the bath nor to wash himself, if he chose; and yet the rare use of water had an effect. If you do not choose to wash with warm water, wash with cold.

Epictetus, About Purity,
The Discourses of Epictetus, c 95

WITCHES exhale a stench from the mouth, the whole body, which is communicated to their garments and fills their houses and the vicinity and infects those who approach. We can attribute this to the secretion of a malodorous animal oil, within the organism, arising from the impure ardors which consume them.

J.J. von Görres, La Mystique Divine,
Naturel et Diabolique, 1861

TRANIO, I saw her coral lips to move
And with her breath she did perfume the air.
Sacred and sweet was all I saw in her.

William Shakespeare,
The Taming of the Shrew, 1594

"I wonder how it is you have such a fine natural perfume," he said, always in the same abstract, inquiring tone of happiness.

"Haven't all women?" she replied, and the peculiar penetrating twang of a brass reed was again in her voice.

"I don't know," he said, quite untouched. "But you are scented like nuts, new kernels of hazel-nuts, and a touch of opium...". He remained abstractedly breathing her with his open mouth, quite absorbed in her.

"You are so strange," she murmured tenderly, hardly able to control her voice to speak.

"I believe," he said slowly, "I can see the stars moving through your hair. No, keep still, you can't see them." Helena lay obediently very still. "I thought I could watch them travelling, crawling like gold flies on the ceiling," he continued in a slow sing-song. "But now you make your hair tremble, and the stars rush about."

D.H. Lawrence, The Trespasser, 1912

ALL thy garments smell of myrrh, and aloes, and cassia, out of the ivory palaces, whereby they have made thee glad.

Psalm 45, King James Version of the Bible, 1611

here's to opening and upward, to leaf and to sap
and to your(in my arms flowering so new)
self whose eyes smell of the sound of rain

E. E. Cummings, No Thanks, 41, 1935

CHAPTER II

"I smell the blood of a British man"

National Bouquets

CHILD Rowland to the dark tower came,
His word was still "Fie, foh, and fum,
I smell the blood of a British man."

William Shakespeare, King Lear, 1605

THE first condition of right thought is right sensation – the first condition of understanding a foreign country is to smell it.

T.S. Eliot, Rudyard Kipling, 1941

A period of bad weather had settled down upon Gardencourt; the days grew shorter, and there was an end to the pretty tea-parties on the lawn. But Isabel had long in-door conversations with her fellow-visitor, and in spite of the rain the two ladies often sallied forth for a walk, equipped with the defensive apparatus which the English climate and the English genius have between them brought to such perfection. Madame Merle was very appreciative; she liked almost everything, including the English rain. "There is always a little of it and never too much at once," she said; "and it never wets you, and it always smells good." She declared that in England the pleasures of smell were great – that in this inimitable island there was a certain mixture of fog and beer and soot which, however odd it might sound, was the national aroma, and was most agreeable to the nostril; and she used to lift the sleeve of her British overcoat and bury her nose in it, to inhale the clear, fine odour of the wool.

Henry James, The Portrait of a Lady, 1881

The winter evening settles down
  With smell of steaks in passageways.
Six o'clock.
The burnt-out ends of smoky days.
And now a gusty shower wraps
The grimy scraps
Of withered leaves about your feet
And newspapers from vacant lots;
The showers beat
On broken blinds and chimney-pots,
And at the corner of the street
A lonely cab-horse steams and stamps.

And then the lighting of the lamps.

II

The morning comes to consciousness
Of faint stale smells of beer
From the sawdust-trampled street
With all its muddy feet that press
To early coffee-stands.

T.S. Eliot, Preludes, 1917

WITH the moon riding so high, the stars now were but a pricking of the grape-coloured sky; the scent from the reedy banks and the river fields, after a whole week of warmth, mounted to his nostrils, sweet and a little rank. It brought a sudden wave of sheer sex-longing – so often and so long had he dreamed of Clare and himself in love on this winding field-scented stream... He remembered the thrill he had felt six months ago, seeing again English grass!... He turned over on to his face and laid his cheek to that grass. There he got the scent better – not sweet, not bitter, but fresh, intimate and delighting, a scent apprehended from his earliest childhood – the scent of England.

John Galsworthy, Over the River, 1933

THERE is nothing on earth more terrible than English music, except English painting. They have no sense of sound, or eye for colour, and I sometimes wonder whether their sense of smell is not equally blunted and dulled: I should not be surprised if they cannot even distinguish between the smell of a ball of horse-dung and an orange.

Heinrich Heine, Lutezia, 1854

ELEANOR sat back under the shade of her white umbrella. The air seemed to hum with heat. The air seemed to smell of soap and chemicals. How thoroughly people wash in England, she thought, looking at the yellow soap, the green soap, and the pink soap in the chemist's window. In Spain she had hardly washed at all.

Virginia Woolf, The Years, 1937

THE Chinese people have always had a very high sense of smell, as is evident in their appreciation of tea and wine and food. In the absence of tobacco, they had developed the art of burning incense, which in Chinese literature was always classified in the same category, and mentioned in the same breath, with tea and wine... In books on the art of living, sections have always been devoted to a discussion of the varieties and quality and preparation of incense.

Lin Yutang, The Importance of Living, 1938

* * *

There is another side to China's fantastic growth: that is the immense toll it is taking on China's environment.

I'll give you an example.

Every night, I leave the BBC office in the centre of Beijing and head home on the airport expressway.

About half way along there's a spot where the car is suddenly enveloped by a thick black blanket of smog. Some nights it is so dense I'm forced to slow down. The car fills with the acrid smell of sulphur.

This is the smell of Beijing in winter. Indeed, it's the smell of China. The smell is of burning coal – millions and millions of tonnes of black sulphurous coal.

My parents used to describe London's pea soup smogs of the 1950s, but I had no idea what they meant. Until I moved to Beijing.

Rupert Wingfield-Hayes,
BBC correspondent, Beijing, 2006

ONE day when Kowanerk [an Inuit woman] and I were alone, she looked up from the boot she was mending to ask, without preamble,

"Do we smell?"

"Yes."

"Does the odour offend you?"

"Yes."

She sewed in silence for a while, then said, "You smell and it's offensive to us. We wondered if we smelled and if it offended you."

Edmund Carpenter, Eskimo Realities, 1973

CERTAIN tribes and races of people have characteristic odors. Negroes have a rank ammoniacal odor, unmitigated by cleanliness; according to Pruner-Bey it is due to a volatile oil set free by the sebaceous follicles. The Esquimaux and Greenlanders have the odors of their greasy and oily foods, and it is said that the Cossacks, who live much with their horses, and who are principally vegetarians, will leave the atmosphere charged with odors several hours after their passage in numbers through a neighbourhood. The lower race of Chinamen are distinguished by a peculiar musty odor, which may be noticed in the laundry shops of this country. Some people, such as the low grade of Indians, have odors, not distinctive, and solely due to the filth of their persons.

Gould and Pyle, Anomalies and Curiosities of Medicine, 1897

THE refined olfactory sense is reflected in the Chinese cuisine and in the fact that, in Peking, one speaks of kissing a baby as "smelling" a baby, which is what is done actually. The Chinese literary language has also many equivalents of the French *odeur de femme*, like "flesh odour" and "fragrance from marble" (a woman's body).

Lin Yutang, My Country and My People, 1936

FLUSH wandered off into the streets of Florence to enjoy the rapture of smell. He threaded his path through main streets and back streets, though squares and alleys, by smell. He nosed his way from smell to smell; the rough, the smooth, the dark, the golden. He went in and out, up and down, where they beat brass, where they bake bread, where the women sit combing their hair, where the bird-cages are piled high on the causeway, where the wine spills itself in dark red stains on the pavement, where leather smells and harness and garlic, where cloth is beaten, where vine leaves tremble, where men sit and drink and spit and dice – he ran in and out, always with his nose to the ground, drinking in the essence; or with his nose in the air vibrating with the aroma. He slept in this hot patch of sun – how sun made the stone reek! he sought that tunnel of shade – how acid shade made the stone smell! He devoured whole bunches of ripe grapes largely because of their purple smell; he chewed and spat out whatever tough relic of goat or macaroni the Italian housewife had thrown from the balcony – goat and macaroni were raucous smells, crimson smells.

Virginia Woolf, Flush, 1933

It is not the contrast of pigstyes and palaces that I complain of, the distinction between the old and new; what I object to is the want of any such striking contrast, but an almost uninterrupted succession of narrow, vulgar-looking streets, where the smell of garlick prevails over the odour of antiquity, with the dingy, melancholy flat fronts of modern-built houses, that seem in search of an owner. A dunghill, an outhouse, the weeds growing under an imperial arch offended me not; but what has a greengrocer's stall, a stupid English china warehouse, a putrid trattoria, a barber's sign, and old clothes or old picture shops or a Gothic palace, with two or three lacqueys in modern liveries lounging at the gate, to do with ancient Rome?

William Hazlitt,
Notes of a Journey through France and Italy, 1826

A NY first-time traveller to Europe is immediately taken by
its smells. The fragrances of garlic, fish, and olive oil all
waft through the streets, carried along by Mediterranean breezes.
These, of course, are the pleasant odors. There also lurks among
the cobbled stones and quaint buildings quite a different smell
– sewer gas. In old cities you have old sewer systems. Old sewer
systems belch gas. This wouldn't be a problem if it weren't for the
fact that eating on the street is so popular and so enjoyable. In
Pisa I remember being almost bowled over by an invisible cloud
of gas on the periphery of a pastry shop where delicate flavours
and subtle fragrances were the foundations of delight. In Napflion
in Greece, Nancy and I frequented a street of restaurants. Each
of these eateries served delicious food. All of them were close
enough to sewer outlets that, depending on the wind, could cause
considerable interference with one's dining enjoyment.

Daniel Pukstas, Traveling with Athena:
A Blind Man's Odyssey through Italy and Greece, 2003

THE issue of cleanliness comes up again and again when French people and Americans come together. Americans complain that the French don't wash enough, while the French find that Americans are overly concerned with germs. While the French palate has developed to a point where it can taste a certain wine and determine what side of the mountain the grapes grew on, the American nose seems to be particularly sensitive to body odors. Proverbs such as "Cleanliness is next to godliness" suggest the almost sacramental nature of hygiene for Americans. Not surprisingly, American companies have developed a vast array of products to help people avoid offending others.

French people feel that a little natural odor is not necessarily objectionable. While France remains the world leader in fine perfumes, the idea of using deodorant to mask normal body odor has still not gained wide acceptance. In a European survey, researchers found that the French are among the most resistant to deodorant – only half of those surveyed use it – although they were close to average in their consumption of soap. Despite the gradual disappearance of the famous bidet in the home, the average French person takes one bath and 4.4 showers a week, making him or her one of the best-washed Europeans. Until they come to the United States, the French simply do not realise that natural body smell can be a serious problem. Therefore, Americans in France may simply have to adapt.

Giles Asselin, Ruth Mastron,
Au Contraire: Figuring Out the French, 2000

Wednesday, December 5, 1917
Pau and Arcachon, France

ONE of the worst features [of French trains] is the odors. I believe the French are the dirtiest people. I have smelled more unpleasant and unnecessary odors in France than in years at home. They are filthy.

Marine Flyer in France,
The Diary of Captain Alfred A. Cunningham, Nov 1917-Jan 1918

AT Colmiers la Haut we were confronted with the first necessity always to be found in every French town – that of cleaning up the town. It was a small village of some 200 population, but there was more filth and dirt to the person than in any place ever seen by me. The cows and horses trailed through the streets of the place, early in the morning and late in the evening, distributing their dung as they walked, and before we could drill upon the streets of the town we became scavengers en masse. Back of each residence was a dung pile carefully thrown high by the frugal hands of the Frenchmen, a reeking, stinking, stench-pot, crying out to High Heaven! What a smell! And the French objected when we removed it. Their wealth was measured by the height of their pile!

Corporal Chris Emmett,
Give Way to the Right, 1934

FRANCE is a country of smells. There's something called pourriture noble. Noble rot. It's a fungus. It grows on grapes, draws the water out, concentrates the juice wonderfully, adds its own fungal flavour, and then you make wines like the sweet Sauternes. Paradise. From rotten grapes. The idea that things should be slightly dirty, overripe, slightly fecal is everywhere in France. They like rotten cheese and dirty sheets and unwashed women.

For a perfumer there is no bad smell. All the great French perfumes, every last one, has some ingredient in it that is repulsive, like civet, this hideous and ferociously powerful extract from the butthole of a Chinese tomcat. Beaver pelt oil. Something. Americans dedicate their lives to the notion that shit shouldn't stink. American perfumery is really, well... Americans have an obsessional neurosis about being clean.

Luca Turin in conversation with Chandler Burr,
The Emperor of Scent, 2003

THE smell of a dead skunk seeps into the Discovery, prompting another unresolved question: "Why do you smell a skunk carcass after you've passed it but not before?"

Then the other smells of the trip come wafting back in memory: the steamy industrial smell of St Louis; fresh-cut hay and a tinge of manure in the Farm Belt, startlingly sweet and brief; the Omaha stockyards, overpowering on a hot day; the musty, claustrophobic air of the SAC bunker, like a tomb; smoke in an earth lodge; buffalo which smells like, well, buffalo; dust caking your nose on a back road in Montana; sage pungent after a rain and even the air cleansed by lightning; horse sweat, a smell and a feel, rank and sticky; trout frying in a pan, a smell and a sound, as is an open campfire; snow and pine and cedar in the Bitterroots; sulphur from hot springs; the permeating scent from a pulp mill that makes you wrinkle your nose and look to see if someone else is in the passenger seat; baked air on the Columbia plateau desert; fish and seaweed in the bays near Astoria, fresh and stagnant at the same time.

Dayton Duncan, Out West: A Journey Through
Lewis and Clark's America, 2003

WHEN he turns the two young men are very close. He can smell their unbathed odour like stale garlic. He thinks how Americans always smell different from Indians, even the office babus under their cologne and deodorant. And then he realizes it is his own sweat, his sudden prickly fear he is smelling.

Chitra Banerjee Divakaruni,
The Mistress of Spices, 1997

BUT, just before we turn hard left to the
C N Tower the smell of skunk squeezes
and cools into the car's red velvet interior;
the real, indefatigable smell of welcome
to North America (that must be all around,
drifting through the safe, residential
city certainties). Maybe it had just been
killed by a car or was fighting off a suburban
pet to protect its young. Whatever, we're
happy to have arrived.

Jon Glover, Taxi, 1994

WE instantly recognise the photographs. We have seen
them many times before and know, without a moment's
hesitation, that we are viewing the Lower East Side... If the
photographs could engage our sense of smell, we would pick up
an array of pungent odors. We would smell the garbage, wrinkle
our noses, and feel sorry that these immigrants and their children
had to live that way.

But we would also whiff the stuff of the carts: the roasting
chestnuts, sour pickles, steaming sweet potatoes, and spicy
chickpeas. If only our sense of taste could be activated, we would
sample with pleasure from these foods. Though the food would be
served on greasy paper, handed to us by the vendors' bare hands
(no tongs or plastic gloves to protect us from germs), we would
devour the briny herring, chewy bread, and smoked meats.

Hasia R. Diner, Lower East Side Memories:
A Jewish Place in America, 2002

THE heat in the street was terrible: and the airlessness, the bustle and the plaster, scaffolding, bricks, and dust all about him, and that special Petersburg stench, so familiar to all who are unable to get out of town in summer – all worked painfully upon the young man's already overwrought nerves. The insufferable stench from the pot-houses, which are particularly numerous in that part of the town, and the drunken men whom he met continually, although it was a working day, completed the revolting misery of the picture. An expression of the profoundest disgust gleamed for a moment in the young man's refined face. He was, by the way, exceptionally handsome, above the average in height, slim, well-built, with beautiful dark eyes and dark brown hair. Soon he sank into deep thought, or more accurately speaking into a complete blankness of mind; he walked along not observing what was about him and not caring to observe it. From time to time, he would mutter something, from the habit of talking to himself, to which he had just confessed. At these moments he would become conscious that his ideas were sometimes in a tangle and that he was very weak; for two days he had scarcely tasted food.

Fyodor Dostoyevsky, Crime and Punishment, 1865-66

I felt towards a Burman almost as I felt towards a woman. Like most other races, the Burmese have a distinctive smell – I cannot describe it: it is a smell that makes one's teeth tingle – but this smell never disgusted me. (Incidentally, Orientals say that *we* smell. The Chinese, I believe, say that a white man smells like a corpse. The Burmese say the same – though no Burman was ever rude enough to say so to me.)

George Orwell, The Road to Wigan Pier, 1937

ABOUT seven, he would rise, wrap himself in a long Turkish cloak, light a cheroot, and lean his elbows on the parapet. Thus he would stand, gazing at the city beneath him, apparently entranced... Soon, the whole town would be astir with the cracking of whips, the beating of gongs, cryings to prayer, lashing of mules, and rattle of brass-bound wheels, while sour odours, made from bread fermenting and incense, and spice, rose even to the heights of Pera itself and seemed the very breath of the strident and multicoloured and barbaric population.

Virginia Woolf, Orlando, 1928

AS the last patient disappeared the doctor sank into his chair, fanning his face with the prescription-pad.

"Ach, this heat! Some mornings I think that never will I get the smell of garlic out of my nose! It iss amazing to me how their very blood becomes impregnated with it. Are you not suffocated, Mr Flory? You English have the sense of smell almost too highly developed. What torments you must all suffer in our filthy East!"

"Abandon your noses, all ye who enter here, what? They might write that up over the Suez Canal. You seem busy this morning?"

"Ass ever. Ah but, my friend, how discouraging iss the work of a doctor in this country! These villagers – dirty, ignorant savages! Even to get them to come to hospital iss all we can do, and they will die of gangrene or carry a tumour ass large ass a melon for ten years rather than face the knife. And such medicines ass their own so-called doctors give to them! Herbs gathered under the new moon, tigers' whiskers, rhinoceros horn, urine, menstrual blood! How men can drink such compounds iss disgusting."

George Orwell, Burmese Days, 1934

THE night had closed in rain, and rolling clouds blotted out the lights of the villages in the valley. Forty miles away, untouched by cloud or storm, the white shoulder of Dongo Pa – the Mountain of the Council of the Gods – upheld the evening star. The monkeys sung sorrowfully to each other as they hunted for dry roots in the fern-draped trees, and the last puff of the day-wind brought from the unseen villages the scent of damp wood smoke, hot cakes, dripping undergrowth, and rotting pine-cones. That smell is the true smell of the Himalayas, and if it once gets into the blood of a man he will, at the last, forgetting everything else, return to the Hills to die. The clouds closed and the smell went away, and there remained nothing in all the world except chilling white mists and the boom of the Sutlej River.

Rudyard Kipling, Namgay Doola, 1891

THE billowing burka merges with every other billowing burka. Sky-blue everywhere. She glances at the ground. In the mud she can distinguish dirty shoes from other dirty shoes ... The smell of saffron, garlic, dried pepper and fresh pakora penetrates the stiff material and mingles with sweat, breath and the smell of strong soap. The nylon material is so dense that one can smell one's own breathing.

Asne Seierstad, The Bookseller of Kabul, 2004

EVERY beach of the Isle is transformed. The big rain makes short cuts to the great sea, and the sea chokes the sluices with weeds and spoil, from which the sun distils a scent compounded of flotsam and drift that seems invigorating. At any rate, it may be enjoyed unrestrictedly, and, with a trifle added by imagination, may inspire many a romantic theme. As a tickler of the more subtle qualities of the mind, what is more effective than a pungency – agreeable or disagreeable? And can there be anything to excite unpleasant reminiscences in fresh incense from unpolluted gatherings of sea and shore? On such grounds is the revel in a hearty wet season founded.

Flowers are few, but the freshly-fallen and decaying leaves underfoot give forth an odour rich and varied; one must stop occasionally to fill the lungs with so potent and pleasant a balsam, and to give thanks for enjoying it on such a generous scale. All the air is saturated with its invigorating principles. Gums and wattles, the huge-leaved "gin-gee," tea-trees, the ripe, orange-tinted fruit of the pandanus along the gullies, the big spreading figs on the edge of the jungle, the pungent native ginger, the full-fruited nutmeg, the few last flowers of the milkwood, the resiniferous gum of the "tangebah," the patchouli-like ixora, and the sodden grass – all contribute to the medley of perfumes, and create a longing for some magic art by which the combination could be fixed, materialized, and sent to those who may still believe that Australia is a scentless land.

E.J. Banfield, Last Leaves from Dunk Island, 1925

THAT February, Delhi seemed like a paradise. Olivia and I filled the garden on our roof terraces with palms and lilies and hollyhocks and we wove bougainvillea through the trellising. The plants which seemed to have died during the winter's cold – the snapdragon, the hibiscus and the frangipani – miraculously sprang back to life and back into bloom. The smells began to change: the wood-smoke and the sweet smell of the dung fires gave way to the heady scent of Indian champa and the first bittersweet whiffs of China orange blossom.

William Dalrymple, City of Djinns, 1994

"Please take these things – my parents sent them for you," he lies, hoping they will never guess what happened to their gifts, and hands her the box of tea which she takes with a polite murmur of surprise. As she turns it over in her hands, studying the label with the habitual attention she gives to consumer products, she queries hopefully, "Is it herbal?" Arun opens out the brown shawl. He shakes out the folds, then arranges it carefully about her shoulders. An aroma arises from it, of another land: muddy, grassy, smoky, ashen. It swamps him, like a river, or like a fire.

She looks at him, then at the wool stuff on her shoulders, in incomprehension. She picks a fold of it, and sniffs. Slowly her face spreads into a flush of wonder. "Why, Ahroon," she stammers, "this is just beautiful. Thank you, thank you," she repeats, and puts her hands to her neck to hold the ends of the shawl together.

Anita Desai, Fasting and Feasting, 1999

BOMBAY used to be a beautiful city, a breathable city. During a strike by the taxi drivers, the air pollution comes down by a quarter from its usual level. They are marvellous January days, when everybody goes out to breathe luxuriously. It is a long time since Bombay smelled so sweet in the winter. Breathing the air in Bombay now is the equivalent of smoking two and a half packets of cigarettes a day. The sun used to set into the sea; now it sets into the smog ...

I couldn't use the public toilets. I tried, once. There were two rows of toilets. Each of them had masses of shit, overflowing out of the toilets and spread liberally all around the cubicle. For the next few hours that image and that stench stayed with me: when I ate, when I drank. It's not merely an aesthetic discomfort; typhoid runs rampant through the slum and spreads through oral-faecal contact. Pools of stagnant water, which are everywhere, breed malaria. Many children also have jaundice. Animal carcasses are spread out on the counters of butchers' shops, sprinkled with flies like a moving spice. The whole slum is pervaded by a stench that I stopped noticing after a while.

Suketu Mehta, Maximum City, 2004

CHAPTER III

"A woman who doesn't wear

perfume has no future"

The Smell Industry

"WHERE should one use perfume?" a young woman asked. "Wherever one wants to be kissed," I said.

Attributed to Coco Chanel, c1925

LA langoureuse Asie et la brûlante Afrique,
Toute un monde lointain, absent, Presque défunt,
Vit dans tes profondeurs, forêt aromatique!
Comme d'autres esprits voguent sur la musique,
Le mien, ô mon amour! nage sur ton parfum.

[*Languorous Asia and burning Africa, a whole world, distant, absent, which has almost ceased to be, lives in your depths, scented forest! As other minds float on music, mine, o my love, swims on your perfume.*]

Charles Baudelaire, La Chevelure, 1857

CES serments, ces parfums, ces baisers infinis,
Renaîtront-ils d'un gouffre interdit à nos sondes,
Comme montent au ciel les soleils rajeunis
Après s'être lavés au fond des mers profondes?
- O serments! ô parfums! ô baisers infinis!

[*Those promises, those perfumes, those endless kisses, will they be born again from deeps our plumb-lines cannot reach, as the rejuvenated suns rise up to heaven, having washed themselves in the depths of the seas? O promises, perfumes, endless kisses!*]

Charles Baudelaire, Le Balcon, 1857

IT is the unseen, unforgettable, ultimate accessory of fashion....
that heralds your arrival and prolongs your departure.

Coco Chanel, Herald Tribune, 1964

IN 1921 she launched her first perfume, Chanel No. 5, reputedly
her lucky number. No. 5 was a mixture of over 80 ingredients
blended by the eminent French chemist, Ernest Beaux, who
owned a laboratory in Grasse... Beaux was at the forefront of the
development of synthetic perfumes, using aldehydes to enhance
the fragrance of costly natural ingredients such as jasmine, which
is the base of No. 5.

Chanel designed the pharmaceutical, Modernist style bottle
for No. 5 herself. Chanel No. 5 was the first perfume to bear a
couturier's name on the label. Both this and the simple name of
her fragrance were a far cry from the exotic names and decorative
flacons which had characterised perfume in the pre-war years...
Chanel returned to Paris with samples of Chanel No. 5, some of
which she atomised in her fitting rooms. When her friends and
clients asked if they could purchase it she claimed she had just
had a small amount made for gifts, but if they thought it would
sell she would market it.

Amy de la Haye and Shelley Tobin,
Chanel, the Couturiere at Work, 1994

"WHAT do you wear in the morning?"
"A sweater and skirt."
"And in the afternoon?"
"Another sweater, another skirt."
"What about the evening?"
"The same, but in silk."
"And at night?"
"Five drops of Chanel No. 5."

Marilyn Monroe, Interview, 1954

COCO CHANEL TO ERNEST BEAUX

"I don't want hints of roses, of lilies of the valley, I want a perfume that is composed. It's a paradox. On a woman, a natural flower scent smells artificial. Perhaps a natural perfume must be created artificially."

*

"When someone offers me a flower, I can smell the hands that picked them."

*

"That's what I expected. A perfume unlike any other ever made. A woman's perfume, redolent, evocative of woman."

*

"Put even more jasmine in it. I want to make it the world's most expensive perfume."

Axel Madsen, Coco Chanel, 1990

CHANEL No. 5, to me, is still the ideal scent for a woman. She can wear it anywhere, anytime, and everybody – husbands, beaus, taxi drivers – everybody loves it. No one has gone beyond Chanel No. 5.

Diane Vreeland, editor of the American Vogue, 1953

YOU always have an image in your head. You can actually smell the accords, which are like musical chords. Perfumery is closely related to music. You will have simple fragrances, simple accords made from two or three items, and it will be like a two or three piece band. And then you have a multiple accord put together, and it becomes a big modern orchestra. In a strange way, creating a fragrance is similar to composing music, because there is also a similarity in finding the "proper" accords. You don't want anything being overpowering. You want it to be harmonious. One of the most important parts of putting a creation together is harmony. You could have layers of notes coming through the fragrance, but yet you still feel it's pleasing. If the fragrance is not layered properly, you'll have parts and pieces sticking out, it will make you uncomfortable, something will disturb you about it. A fragrance that's not well balanced is not well accepted... When I first saw Picasso's Guernica, it was disturbing. I was horrified and fascinated at the same time. It was disturbing, but also deeply moving. Perfumes do that, too – shock and fascinate us. They disturb us. Our lives are quiet. We like to be disturbed by delight.

Sophia Grojsman, perfumer, quoted in Diane Ackerman,
A Natural History of the Senses, 1990

THE barge she sat in, like a burnish'd throne,
Burnt on the water. The poop was beaten gold,
Purple the sails, and so perfumed that
The winds were love-sick with them; the oars were silver,
Which to the tune of flutes kept stroke, and made
The water which they beat to follow faster,
As amorous of their strokes.

William Shakespeare,
Antony and Cleopatra, 1607

SHE left the smell of perfume on my hand

Josephine Coll describing the visit of Princess Diana
to the Henry Street Settlement on the Lower East Side of Manhattan,
New York Times, 1989

STILL to be neat, still to be drest,
As you were going to a feast;
Still to be powdered, still perfumed :
Lady, it is to be presumed,
Though Art's hid causes are not found,
All is not sweet, all is not sound.

Give me a look, give me a face,
That makes simplicity a grace;
Robes loosely flowing, hair as free:
Such sweet neglect more taketh me,
Than all the adulteries of Art;
They strike mine eyes, but not my heart.

Ben Jonson, Epicoene, 1609

THE idea is to make the woman so repulsive that the attacker
runs away. It sounds funny until you smell it.

On perfume for protection against assaults,
Wall Street Journal, 1985

ITS aromatic substances lull to sleep, allay anxieties, and brighten dreams. It is made of things that delight most in the night.

Plutarch on the Egyptian perfume Kyphi,
Isis and Osiris, c100

THESE perfumes form the objects of a luxury which may be looked upon as being the most superfluous of any, for pearls and jewels, after all, do pass to a man's representative, and garments have some durability; but unguents lose their odour in an instant, and die away the very hour they are used. The very highest recommendation of them is, that when a female passes by, the odour which proceeds from her may possibly attract the attention of those even who till then are intent upon something else. In price they exceed so large a sum even as four hundred denarii per pound: so vast is the amount that is paid for a luxury made not for our own enjoyment, but for that of others; for the person who carries the perfume about him is not the one, after all, that smells it.

Pliny, The Natural History, c77

YOU will dine well, dear Fabullus, at my place
In a few days, if the gods are kind to you,
If you bring along with you a dinner large,
And splendid, and yes, a charming girl as well,
And wine and wit and every kind of laughter.
If, I say, you bring along these things, sweet friend,
You will dine well. For you Catullus' wallet
Is full of dust and cobwebs. But in return
You will receive the purest essence of love
Or something still more fragrant and more graceful:
For I'll provide a perfume which was given
To my girl by the Venuses and Cupids.
When you get to smell it, you will ask the gods
To make you, dear Fabullus, entirely nose.

Catullus, Poem 13, c54 BC

A woman who doesn't wear perfume has no future

Attributed to Paul Valéry, c1920

BUT, good heavens! Nowadays some people actually put scent
in their drinks and it is worth the bitter flavour for their body
to enjoy the lavish scent both inside and outside.

Pliny, The Natural History, c77

THEN Jesus six days before the passover came to Bethany, where Lazarus was which had been dead, whom he raised from the dead. There they made him a supper; and Martha served: but Lazarus was one of them that sat at the table with him. Then took Mary a pound of ointment of spikenard, very costly, and anointed the feet of Jesus, and wiped his feet with her hair: and the house was filled with the odour of the ointment. Then saith one of his disciples, Judas Iscariot, Simon's son, which should betray him, Why was not this ointment sold for three hundred pence, and given to the poor? This he said, not that he cared for the poor; but because he was a thief, and had the bag, and bare what was put therein. Then said Jesus, Let her alone: against the day of my burying hath she kept this. For the poor always ye have with you; but me ye have not always.

John, chapter 8, King James Version of the Bible, 1611

THERE was a woman who was taken in adultery. We are not told the history of her love, but that love must have been very great; for Jesus said that her sins were forgiven her, not because she repented, but because her love was so intense and wonderful. Later on, a short time before his death, as he sat at a feast, the woman came in and poured costly perfumes on his hair. His friends tried to interfere with her, and said that it was an extravagance, and that the money that the perfume cost should have been expended on charitable relief of people in want, or something of that kind. Jesus did not accept that view. He pointed out that the material needs of Man were great and very permanent, but that the spiritual needs of Man were greater still, and that in one divine moment, and by selecting its own mode of expression, a personality might make itself perfect. The world worships the woman, even now, as a saint.

Oscar Wilde, The Soul of Man under Socialism, 1891

HIS teeth were set on edge. He would have liked to spit. Simultaneously with the woman in the basement kitchen he thought of Katharine, his wife. Winston was married – had been married, at any rate: probably he still was married, so far as he knew his wife was not dead. He seemed to breathe again the warm stuffy odour of the basement kitchen, an odour compounded of bugs and dirty clothes and villainous cheap scent, but nevertheless alluring, because no woman of the Party ever used scent, or could be imagined as doing so. Only the proles used scent. In his mind the smell of it was inextricably mixed up with fornication.

George Orwell, *Nineteen Eighty-four, 1949*

A moment later he was inside the room. He opened the green suit-case; and all at once he was breathing Lenina's perfume, filling his lungs with her essential being... [he] kissed a perfumed acetate handkerchief... Opening a box, he spilt a cloud of scented powder. His hands were floury with the stuff. He wiped them on his chest, on his shoulders, on his bare arms. Delicious perfume! He shut his eyes; he rubbed his cheek against his own powdered arm. Touch of smooth skin against his face, scent in his nostrils of musky dust – her real presence. "Lenina," he whispered, "Lenina!"

Aldous Huxley, *Brave New World, 1932*

THE courtesans of nineteenth-century Paris were quick to realise that musk had for centuries been regarded in the East as a powerful aphrodisiac and provided themselves with a small bag of it, which they carried between their breasts, ostensibly to conceal unwanted body odour but in effect to encourage trade.

Michael Stoddart, The Scented Ape, 1990

CIVET will cause so much desire for coitus that she will almost continually wish to make love with her husband. And in particular, if a man wishes to go with a woman, if he shall place on his penis of this same civet and unexpectedly use it, he will arouse in her the greatest of pleasure.

Petrus Castellus, De Hyaena Odorifera, 1688

BORELLUS gives the history of a man who before coitus rubbed his virile member with musk, and, similar to the connection of a dog and bitch, was held fast in his wife's vagina; it was only after the injection of great quantities of water to soften the parts that separation was obtained. Diemerbroeck confirms this singular property of musk by an analogous observation, in which the ludicrous method of throwing cold water on the persons was practised.

Gould and Pyle, Anomalies and
Curiosities of Medicine, Philadelphia, 1897

I cannot talk with civet in the room,
A fine puss-gentleman that's all perfume.

William Cowper, Conversation, 1782

INTERESTINGLY, the use of perfume by men, once widespread in the West, declined with the rise of the machine at the time of the Industrial Revolution. It might be that, for men to enter into the new world of the mechanical other, they had to renounce the fragrances which are metaphorically antithetical to the symbolic inodorateness of the barren, insensible machine. This metaphorical opposition between fragrance and machinery may also explain in part why our modern media (such as television and computers) are so tellingly devoid of odours. In any case, machines are classified as inodorate in Western culture not only because they in fact tend to be made of materials which give off little odour, but because their sterility makes them symbolically inodorate. Nothing more absurd than a perfumed machine. The robot is neither fragrant nor foul. Its otherness is the otherness not simply of anti-culture but of anti-life.

Constance Classen, Worlds of Sense:
Exploring the Senses in History and Across Cultures, 1993

EPIGRAPHS in an undecipherable language, half their letters rubbed away by the sand-laden wind: this is what you will be, O parfumeries, for the noseless man of the future. You will still open your doors to us, your carpets will still muffle our footsteps, you will receive us in your jewel-box space, with no jutting corners, the walls of lacquered wood, and shopgirls or patronnes, colourful and soft as artificial flowers, will let their plump arms, wielding atomizers, graze us, or the hem of their skirts, as they stand tip-toe on stools, reaching upwards. But the phials, the ampules, the jars with their spire-like or cut-glass stoppers will weave in vain from shelf to shelf their network of harmonies, assonances, dissonances, counterpoints, modulations, cadenzas: our deaf nostrils will no longer catch the notes of their scale. We will not distinguish musk from verbena: amber and mignonette, bergamot and bitter-almond will remain mute, sealed in the calm slumber of their bottles. When the olfactory alphabet, which made them so many words in a precious lexicon, is forgotten, perfumes will be left speechless, inarticulate, illegible.

Italo Calvino, The Name, The Nose, 1972

HE had long been skilled in the science of smell. He believed that this sense could give one delights equal to those of hearing and sight; each sense being susceptible, if naturally keen and if properly cultivated, to new impressions, which it could intensify, coordinate and compose into that unity which constitutes a creative work. And it was not more abnormal and unnatural that an art should be called into existence by disengaging odours than that another art should be evoked by detaching sound waves or by striking the eye with diversely coloured rays.

In this art, the branch devoted to achieving certain effects by artificial methods particularly delighted him. Perfumes, in fact, rarely come from the flowers whose names they bear. The artist who dared to borrow nature's elements would only produce a bastard work which would have neither authenticity nor style, inasmuch as the essence obtained by the distillation of flowers would bear but a distant and vulgar relation to the odour of the living flower, wafting its fragrance into the air.

Thus, with the exception of the inimitable jasmine which it is impossible to counterfeit, all flowers are perfectly represented by the blend of aromatic spirits, stealing the very personality of the model, and to it adding that nuance the more, that heady scent, that rare touch which entitled a thing to be called a work of art.

To resume, in the science of perfumery, the artist develops the natural odour of the flowers, working over his subject like a jeweller refining the lustre of a gem and making it precious.

Little by little, the arcana of this art, most neglected of all, was revealed to Des Esseintes who could now read this language, as diversified and insinuating as that of literature, this style with its unexpected concision under its vague flowing appearance.

To achieve this end he had first been compelled to master the grammar and understand the syntax of odours, learning the secret of the rules that regulate them, and, once familiarized with the dialect, he compared the works of the masters, of the Atkinsons and Lubins, the Chardins and Violets, the Legrands and Piesses; then he separated the construction of their phrases, weighed the value of their words and the arrangement of their periods.

Later on, in this idiom of fluids, experience was able to support theories too often incomplete and banal.

Classic perfumery, in fact, was scarcely diversified, almost colourless and uniformly issuing from the mould cast by the ancient chemists. It was in its dotage, confined to its old alambics, when the romantic period was born and had modified the old style, rejuvenating it, making it more supple and malleable.

Step by step, its history followed that of our language. The perfumed Louis XIII style, composed of elements highly prized at that time, of iris powder, musk, chive and myrtle water already designated under the name of "water of the angels," was hardly sufficient to express the cavalier graces, the rather crude tones of the period which certain sonnets of Saint-Amand have preserved for us. Later, with myrrh and olibanum, the mystic odours, austere and powerful, the pompous gesture of the great period, the redundant artifices of oratorial art, the full, sustained harmonious style of Bossuet and the masters of the pulpit were almost possible. Still later, the sophisticated, rather bored graces of French society under Louis XV, more easily found their interpretation in the almond which in a manner summed up this epoch; then, after the ennui and jadedness of the first empire, which misused Eau de Cologne and rosemary, perfumery rushed, in the wake of Victor Hugo and Gautier, towards the Levant. It created oriental combinations, vivid Eastern nosegays, discovered new intonations, antitheses which until then had been unattempted, selected and made use of antique nuances which it complicated, refined and assorted. It resolutely rejected that voluntary decrepitude to which it had been reduced by the Malesherbes, the Boileaus, the Andrieuxes and the Baour-Lormians, wretched distillers of their own poems.

But this language had not remained stationery since the period of 1830. It had continued to evolve and, patterning itself on the progress of the century, had advanced parallel with the other arts. It, too, had yielded to the desires of amateurs and artists, receiving its inspiration from the Chinese and Japanese, conceiving fragrant albums, imitating the Takeoka bouquets of flowers, obtaining the odour of Rondeletia from the blend of lavender and clove; the peculiar aroma of Chinese ink from the marriage of patchouli and camphor; the emanation of Japanese Hovenia by compounds of citron, clove and neroli.

Des Esseintes studied and analyzed the essences of these fluids, experimenting to corroborate their texts. He took pleasure in playing the role of a psychologist for his personal satisfaction, in taking apart and re-assembling the machinery of a work, in separating the pieces forming the structure of a compound exhalation, and his sense of smell had thereby attained a sureness that was all but perfect.

Just as a wine merchant has only to smell a drop of wine to recognize the grape, as a hop dealer determines the exact value of hops by sniffing a bag, as a Chinese trader can immediately tell the origin of the teas he smells, knowing in what farms of what mountains, in what Buddhistic convents it was cultivated, the very time when its leaves were gathered, the state and the degree of torrefaction, the effect upon it of its proximity to the plum-tree and other flowers, to all those perfumes which change its essence, adding to it an unexpected touch and introducing into its dryish flavour a hint of distant fresh flowers; just so could Des Esseintes, by inhaling a dash of perfume, instantly explain its mixture and the psychology of its blend, and could almost give the name of the artist who had composed and given it the personal mark of his individual style.

Naturally he had a collection of all the products used by perfumers. He even had the real Mecca balm, that rare balm cultivated only in certain parts of Arabia Petraea and under the monopoly of the ruler.

Now, seated in his dressing room in front of his table, he thought of creating a new bouquet... He worked with amber and with Tonkin musk, marvellously powerful; with patchouli, the most poignant of vegetable perfumes whose flower, in its habitat, wafts an odour of mildew. Try what he would, the eighteenth century obsessed him; the panier robes and furbelows appeared before his eyes; memories of Boucher's "Venus" haunted him; recollections of Themidor's romance, of the exquisite Rosette pursued him. Furious, he rose and to rid himself of the obsession, with all his strength he inhaled that pure essence of spikenard, so dear to Orientals and so repulsive to Europeans because of its pronounced odour of valerian. He was stunned by the violence of the shock. As though pounded by hammer strokes, the filigranes of the delicate odour disappeared; he profited by the period of respite to escape the dead centuries, the antiquated fumes, and to enter, as he formerly had done, less limited or more recent works.

He had of old loved to lull himself with perfumes. He used effects analogous to those of the poets, and employed the admirable order of certain pieces of Baudelaire, such as "Irreparable" and "le Balcon", where the last of the five lines composing the strophe is the echo of the first verse and returns, like a refrain, to steep the soul in infinite depths of melancholy and languor.

He strayed into reveries evoked by those aromatic stanzas, suddenly brought to his point of departure, to the motive of his meditation, by the return of the initial theme, reappearing, at stated intervals, in the fragrant orchestration of the poem.

He actually wished to saunter through an astonishing, diversified landscape, and he began with a sonorous, ample phrase that suddenly opened a long vista of fields for him. With his vaporizers, he injected an essence formed of ambrosia, lavender and sweet peas into this room; this formed an essence which, when distilled by an artist, deserves the name by which it is known: "extract of wild grass"; into this he introduced an exact blend of tuberose, orange flower and almond, and forthwith artificial lilacs sprang into being, while the linden-trees rustled, their thin emanations, imitated by extract of London tilia, drooping earthward.

Into this decor, arranged with a few broad lines, receding as far as the eye could reach, under his closed lids, he introduced a light rain of human and half feline essences, possessing the aroma of petticoats, breathing of the powdered, painted woman, the stephanotis, ayapana, opopanax, champaka, sarcanthus and cypress wine, to which he added a dash of syringa, in order to give to the artificial life of paints which they exhaled, a suggestion of natural dewy laughter and pleasures enjoyed in the open air.

Then, through a ventilator, he permitted these fragrant waves to escape, only preserving the field which he renewed, compelling it to return in his strophes like a ritornello.

The women had gradually disappeared. Now the plain had grown solitary. Suddenly, on the enchanted horizon, factories appeared whose tall chimneys flared like bowls of punch.

The odour of factories and of chemical products now passed with the breeze which was simulated by means of fans; nature exhaled its sweet effluvia amid this putrescence.

Des Esseintes warmed a pellet of storax, and a singular odour, at once repugnant and exquisite, pervaded the room. It partook of the delicious fragrance of jonquil and of the stench of gutta percha and coal oil. He disinfected his hands, inserted his resin in a hermetically sealed box, and the factories disappeared.

Then, among the revived vapours of the lindens and meadow grass, he threw several drops of new mown hay, and, amid this magic site for the moment despoiled of its lilacs, sheaves of hay were piled up, introducing a new season and scattering their fine effluence into these summer odours.

At last, when he had sufficiently enjoyed this sight, he suddenly scattered the exotic perfumes, emptied his vaporizers, threw in his concentrated spirits, poured his balms, and, in the exasperated and stifling heat of the room there rose a crazy sublimated nature, a paradoxical nature which was neither genuine nor charming, reuniting the tropical spices and the peppery breath of Chinese sandal wood and Jamaica hediosmia with the French odours of jasmine, hawthorn and verbena. Regardless of seasons and climates he forced trees of diverse essences into life, and flowers with conflicting fragrances and colours. By the clash of these tones he created a general, nondescript, unexpected, strange perfume in which reappeared, like an obstinate refrain, the decorative phrase of the beginning, the odours of the meadows fanned by the lilacs and lindens.

Suddenly a poignant pain seized him; he felt as though wimbles were drilling into his temples. Opening his eyes he found himself in his dressing room, seated in front of his table. Stupefied, he painfully walked across the room to the window which he half opened. A puff of wind dispelled the stifling atmosphere which was enveloping him. To exercise his limbs, he walked up and down gazing at the ceiling where crabs and sea-wrack stood out in relief against a background as light in colour as the sands of the seashore. A similar decor covered the plinths and bordered the partitions which were covered with Japanese sea-green crepe, slightly wrinkled, imitating a river rippled by the wind. In this light current swam a rose petal, around which circled a school of tiny fish painted with two strokes of the brush.

But his eyelids remained heavy. He ceased to pace about the short space between the baptistery and the bath; he leaned against the window. His dizziness ended.

Joris-Karl Huysmans, Against the Grain, 1884

IT may possibly recur to your memory that when I examined the paper upon which the printed words were fastened I made a close inspection for the water-mark. In doing so I held it within a few inches of my eyes, and was conscious of a faint smell of the scent known as white jessamine. There are seventy-five perfumes, which it is very necessary that a criminal expert should be able to distinguish from each other, and cases have more than once within my own experience depended upon their prompt recognition. The scent suggested the presence of a lady, and already my thoughts began to turn towards the Stapletons. Thus I had made certain of the hound, and had guessed at the criminal before ever we went to the west country.

Arthur Conan Doyle,
The Hound of the Baskervilles, 1902

GOOD authorities declare that Arabia does not produce so large a quantity of perfume in a year's output as was burned by the Emperor Nero in a day at the obsequies of his consort Poppaea. Then reckon up the vast number of funerals celebrated yearly throughout the entire world, and the perfumes such as are given to the gods a grain at a time, that are piled up in heaps to the honour of dead bodies! Yet the gods used not to regard with less favour the worshippers who petitioned them with salted spelt, but rather, as the facts show, they were more benevolent in those days... By the lowest reckoning India, China and the Arabian peninsula take from our empire 100 million sesterces every year – that is the sum which our luxuries and our women cost us; for what fraction of these imports, I ask you, now goes to the gods...

Pliny, The Natural History, c77

WHAT is this sign of respect which comes from the smell of gum of a tree burning in a fire? Does this, do you suppose, give honour to the heavenly magnates? Or if their displeasure has been aroused at any time, is it really soothed and dissipated by incense smoke? But if it is smoke the gods want, why do you not offer them any kind of smoke? Or must it only be incense? If you answer that incense has a nice smell, while other substances have not, tell me if the gods have nostrils, and can they smell with them? But if the gods are incorporeal, odours and perfumes can have no effect at all upon them, since corporeal substances cannot affect incorporeal beings.

Arnobius, Adversus Nationes, c400

AND so he would not study perfumes... He saw that there was no mood of the mind that had not its counterpart in the sensuous life, and set himself to discover their true relations, wondering what there was in frankincense that made one mystical, and in ambergrise that stirred one's passions, and in violets that woke the memory of dead romances, and in musk that troubled the brain, and in champak that stained the imagination; and seeking often to elaborate a real psychology of perfumes, and to estimate the several influences of sweet-smelling roots, and scented pollen-laden flowers, or aromatic balms, and of dark and fragrant woods, of spikenard that sickens, of hovenia that makes men mad, and of aloes that are said to be able to expel melancholy from the soul.

Oscar Wilde, The Picture of Dorian Gray, 1891

NOMBRE Noir ...was, and still is, a radical surprise. A perfume, like the timbre of a voice, can say something quite independent of the words actually spoken. What Nombre Noir said was "flower". But the way it said it was an epiphany. The flower at the core of Nombre Noir was half-way between a rose and a violet, but without a trace of the sweetness of either, set instead against an austere, almost saintly background of cigar-box cedar notes. At the same time, it wasn't dry, and seemed to be glistening with a liquid freshness that made its deep colours glow like a stained-glass window.

The voice of Nombre Noir was that of a child older than its years, at once fresh, husky, modulated and faintly capricious. There was a knowing naivety about it which made me think of Colette's writing style in her Claudine books. It brought to mind a purple ink to write love letters with, and that wonderful French word farouche, which can mean either shy or fierce or a bit of both

. . .

Fougère Royale starts the way some Bruckner symphonies do, with a muted pianissimo of strings, giving an impression of tremendous ease and quiet power. It does smell of coumarin, to be sure, but it is also fresh, clean, austere, almost bitter. This is the reference smell of scrubbed bathrooms, suggestive of black and white tiles, clean, slightly damp towels, a freshly shaven daddy. But wait! There's a funny thing in there, something not altogether pleasant. It's a touch of natural civet, stuff that comes from the rear end of an Asian cat and smells like it does. Suddenly I understand: we're in a bathroom! The idea here is shit, and what's more, someone else's shit, that faint shock of slightly repellent intimacy you get when you go to the loo at someone's dinner party and smell the air. Small wonder Fougère Royale was such a success. At a distance, he who wears it is everyone's favourite son-in-law; up close, a bit of an animal.

Luca Turin, The Secret of Scent,
Adventures in Perfume and the Science of Smell, 2006

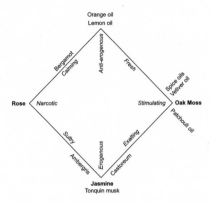

FROM the hair-type diagram it can be seen that at the centre the arc representing the blonde type is at the a-s side of the square which corresponds to perfumes with a fresh effect. This means that perfumes with fresh effect best harmonize with blonde women. In addition, the blonde arc also encompasses the corners a (anti-erogenous) and s (stimulating) as well as large parts of the sides n-a (calming) and s-e (exalting). From this it may be concluded that perfumes with anti-erogenous and stimulating effects also fit this type very well, and that calming and exalting perfumes fit it quite well. Less suitable for blondes are purely narcotic and erogenous perfumes, and sultry perfumes are quite unsuitable: the blonde arc leaves the side e-n completely free.

In the same way, the diagram shows that exalting (e-s) perfumes go best with the redhead type, and sultry (n-e) perfumes with the brunette. Fresh (a-s) perfumes are least suited to the brunette, calming perfumes (n-a) least suited to the redhead.

The brown-haired type occurs widely in the western world, accounting for about 60% of all women. It can be seen as a mixture of blonde and black hair. It is therefore not represented by its own arc but distributed over the sections of the arcs that the brunette and the blonde type have in common. Thus, calming perfumes (n-a) would best harmonize with a "neutral" brown, for darker shades of this type narcotic (n) and sultry (n-e) would be best, and for lighter shades anti-erogenous (a) and fresh (a-s) perfumes.

Paul Jellinek, The Psychological
Basis of Perfumery, 1997

NOW the Chinese live all their lives in the proximity of very nasty smells. They do not notice them. Their nostrils are blunted to the odours that assail the Europeans and so they can move on an equal footing with the tiller of the soil, the coolie, and the artisan. I venture to think that the cess-pool is more necessary to democracy than parliamentary institutions. The invention of the "sanitary convenience" has destroyed the sense of equality in men. It is responsible for class hatred much more than the monopoly of capital in the hands of the few.

It is a tragic thought that the first man who pulled the plug of a water-closet with that negligent gesture rang the knell of democracy.

Somerset Maugham, On a Chinese Screen, 1955

WHILE engaged in this colloquy, they perceived the old matron bring the drugs, so Pao-yü bade her fetch the silver pot, used for boiling medicines in, and then he directed her to prepare the decoction on the brasier.

"The right thing would be," Ch'ing Wen suggested, "that you should let them go and get it ready in the tea-room; for will it ever do to fill this room with the smell of medicines?"

"The smell of medicines," Pao-yü rejoined, "is far nicer than that emitted by the whole lot of flowers. Fairies pick medicines and prepare medicines. Besides this, eminent men and cultured scholars gather medicines and concoct medicines; so that it constitutes a most excellent thing. I was just thinking that there's everything and anything in these rooms and that the only thing that we lack is the smell of medicines; but as luck would have it, everything is now complete."

Cao Xueqin, Hung Lou Meng, 1763

THE first smell to greet you when you enter the tea room is the strong sweet aroma of incense which masks the smell of charcoal. The type known as koboku is used with the brazier, another one, neriko, is used with the fire pit. There are two different ways of burning incense, either directly in the fire (shoko), or placed near the fire and burned slowly (kinko). Sometimes the incense is separated from the fire by a thin piece of mica. This procedure is known as chuko, and is only used on very special occasions. There are also two types of incense burners, one called koro, used to perfume the entire room, and a small one called kikigoro, which is usually picked up by the guests for a fragrant whiff.

Sen'o Tanaka, The Tea Ceremony, 1973

THE benefits of the use of incense are manifold. High-minded recluse scholars, engaged in their discussion of truth and religion, feel that it clears their mind and pleases their spirit when they burn a stick of incense. At the fourth watch of the night, when the solitary moon is hanging in the sky, and one feels cool and detached towards life, it emancipates his heart and enables him to whistle leisurely... When a lady in red pyjamas is standing by your side, and you are holding her hand around the incense-burner and whispering secrets to each other, it warms your heart and intensifies your love. You may therefore call it "the ancient stimulant of passion"... It is also useful for warding off evil smells and the malicious atmosphere of a swamp, useful anywhere and everywhere one goes.

. . .

People nowadays lack the appreciation of true fragrance and go in for strange and exotic names, trying to outdo one another by having a mixture of different kinds, not realising that the fragrance of aloeswood is entirely natural, and that the best of its kind has an indescribable subtlety and mildness.

T'u Long, Desultory Remarks on
Furnishing the Abode of the Retired Scholar, c1600

IN the 1950s, Hans Laube, a Swiss professor of osmics (the study of smells) discovered how to reproduce odors in a movie theater. The invention-which came to be known as Smell-O-Vision!-was introduced in the 1960 film Scent of Mystery.

Did Smell-O-Vision! make olfactory sense? It worked like this: tiny plastic hidden tubes under your seat pumped out smells like garlic, pipe smoke, and shoe-shine wax from a centralized "smell brain."

Like Aldous Huxley's "feelies" in Brave New World, Smell-O-Vision! promised its audience a total immersion in movie illusion. Newspaper advertisements equated its significance to The Jazz Singer: "First They Moved (1895)! Then They Talked (1927)! Now They Smell!"

www.retrofuture.com

CUSTOMERS will probably agree that the smell they liked best was the one they got during intermission: fresh air.

Time Magazine, 1960

ARMCHAIR football fans will now be able to create a stink during the World Cup. England supporters who are unable to get tickets for the tournament in Germany can soak up all the football smells in the comfort of their own home for less than £20.

Dale Air, in Kirham, Lancashire, has designed a range of scents that allows fans to smell the grass of the pitch, the half-time pies, the sweat of the changing rooms or the furniture polish of the trophy room. The pack of four cubes costs £17.61.

The Times, 2006

IN Oakland, Calif., DigiScents, Inc. is developing a digital scent device, called the iSmell. They are fully aware of how people will respond to the device's tongue-in-cheek name... A prototype of the iSmell Personal Scent Synthesizer is shaped like a shark's fin, and it will be connected to your PC through a serial or USB port. It can be plugged into any ordinary electrical outlet. Here's how it works:

DigiScents has indexed thousands of smells based on their chemical structure and their place on the scent spectrum. Each scent is then coded and digitized into a small file. The digital file is embedded in Web content or email. A user requests or triggers the file by clicking a mouse or opening an e-mail. A small amount of the aroma is emitted by the device in the direct vicinity of the user.

The iSmell can create thousands of everyday scents with a small cartridge that contains 128 primary odors. These primary odors are mixed together to generate other smells that closely replicate common natural and manmade odors. The scent cartridge, like a printer's toner cartridge, will have to be replaced periodically to maintain the scent accuracy.

TriSenx is planning to take you one step further, by allowing users to not only download scents, but to print out flavors that can be tasted. The Savannah, Ga., based company has developed a patented technology that allows users to print smells onto thick fiber paper sheets and taste specific flavors by licking the paper coated with the smell.

The SENX machine is a printer-like desktop device that will produce smells based on data programmed into a Web page. SENX stands for Sensory Enhanced Net eXperience. Like the iSmell, the SENX machine will be activated by user actions. The fragrances and aromas are stored in a disposable cartridge within the SENX. This cartridge has 20 chambers, each holding a distinct scent. Thousands of smells can be created with a 20-chamber cartridge and a 40-palette rendition, which composes two separate cartridges.

http://computer.howstuffworks.com/internet-odor3.htm

CHAPTER IV

"The farting,

panting,

drooling,

barking,

shitting

beast"

Odoriferous Animals

HERE, then, the biographer must perforce come to a pause. Where two or three thousand words are insufficient for what we see – and Mrs. Browning had to admit herself beaten by the Apennines: "Of these things I cannot give you any idea," she admitted – there are no more than two words and perhaps one-half for what we smell. The human nose is practically non-existent. The greatest poets in the world have smelt nothing but roses on the one hand, and dung on the other. The infinite gradations that lie between are unrecorded. Yet it was in the world of smell that Flush mostly lived. Love was chiefly smell; form and colour were smell; music and architecture, law, politics and science were smell. To him religion itself was smell. To describe his simplest experience with the daily chop or biscuit is beyond our power. Not even Mr. Swinburne could have said what the smell of Wimpole Street meant to Flush on a hot afternoon in June. As for describing the smell of a spaniel mixed with the smell of torches, laurels, incense, banners, wax candles and a garland of rose leaves crushed by a satin heel that has been laid up in camphor, perhaps Shakespeare, had he paused in the middle of writing Antony and Cleopatra – But Shakespeare did not pause. Confessing our inadequacy, then, we can but note that to Flush Italy, in these the fullest, the freest, the happiest years of his life, meant mainly a succession of smells. Love, it must be supposed, was gradually losing its appeal. Smell remained.

Virginia Woolf, Flush, 1933

DE sa fourrure blonde et brune
Sort un parfum si doux, qu'un soir
J'en fus embaumé, pour l'avoir
Caressée une fois, rien qu'une.

[From his blond and brown fur comes a smell so sweet that one evening I was all perfumed with it after having stroked him once, just once.]

Charles Baudelaire, Le Chat, 1857

Stephen D, aged 22, medical student, on highs (cocaine, PCP, chiefly amphetamines)

VIVID dream one night, dreamt he was a dog, in a world unimaginably rich and significant in smells. ("The happy smell of water... the brave smell of a stone.") Waking, he found himself in just such a world.... it was the exaltation of smell which really transformed his world: "I had dreamt I was a dog – it was an olfactory dream – a world in which all other sensations, enhanced as they were, paled before smell." And with all this there went a sort of trembling, eager emotion, and a strange nostalgia, as of a lost world, half-forgotten, half recalled.

"I went into a scent shop," he continued. "I had never had much of a nose for smells before, but now I distinguished each one instantly – and I found each one unique, evocative, a whole world." He found he could distinguish all his friends – and patients – by smell: "I went into the clinic, I sniffed like a dog, and in that sniff recognised, before seeing them, the twenty patients who were there. Each had his own olfactory physiognomy, a smell-face, far more vivid and evocative, more redolent, than any sight face." He could smell their emotions – fear, contentment, sexuality – like a dog. He could recognise every street, every shop, by smell – he could find his way around New York, infallibly, by smell.

He experienced a certain impulse to sniff and touch everything ("It wasn't really real until I felt it and smelt it") but suppressed this, when with others, lest he seem inappropriate. Sexual smells were exciting and increased – but no more so, he felt, than food smells and other smells. Smell pleasure was intense – smell displeasure, too – but it seemed to him less a world of mere pleasure and displeasure than a whole aesthetic, a whole judgement, a whole new significance, which surrounded him. "It was a world overwhelmingly concrete, of particulars," he said, "a world overwhelming in immediacy, in immediate significance."...

Rather suddenly, after three weeks, this strange transformation ceased – his sense of smell, all his senses, returned to normal; he found himself back, with a sense of mingled loss and relief, in his old world of pallor, sensory faintness, non-concreteness and abstraction. "I'm glad to be back," he said, "but it's a tremendous loss, too. I see now what we give up in being civilised and human. We need the other – the "primitive" – as well... It was like a visit to another world, a world of pure perception, rich, alive, self-sufficient and full. If only I could go back sometimes and be a dog again!"

Oliver Sacks, The Man who
Mistook his Wife for a Hat, 1985

WHEN my friend takes her German shepherd Jackie out for a walk, Jackie sniffs at curb, rock, and tree, and soon senses what dog has been there, its age, sex, mood, health, when it last passed by. For Jackie, it's like reading the gossip column of the morning newspaper. The lane reveals its invisible trails to her nose as it doesn't to her owner. She will add her scent to the quilt of scents on a tuft of grass, and the next dog that comes along will read, in the aromatic hieroglyphics of the neighbourhood, Jackie, 5.00pm, young female, on hormone therapy because of a bladder ailment, well fed, cheerful, seeks a friend.

Diane Ackerman,
A Natural History of the Senses, 1990

"NICE dog, good dog, dear doggie, come and smell some excellent scent from the best shop in town."

And the dog, wagging its tail, which is, I think, in these poor creatures, the sign corresponding to laughter or smiling, comes up and applies its wet nose, curiously, to the open bottle; then, starting back in fear, barks at me reproachfully.

"Wretched dog! If I had offered you a pile of excrement, you would have sniffed it delightedly and perhaps eaten it. Thus even you, unworthy companion of my unhappy life, are like the public, to whom one must never offer delicate scents which enrage it, but carefully selected ordure."

Charles Baudelaire,
The Dog and the Scent Bottle, 1869

WE others, who have long lost the more subtle of the physical senses, have not even proper terms to express an animal's inter-communications with his surroundings, living or otherwise, and have only the word "smell", for instance, to include the whole range of delicate thrills which murmur in the nose of the animal night and day, summoning, warning, inciting, repelling. It was one of these mysterious fairy calls from out the void that suddenly reached Mole in the darkness, making him tingle through and through with its very familiar appeal, even while yet he could not clearly remember what it was. He stopped dead in his tracks, his nose searching hither and thither in its efforts to recapture the fine filament, the telegraphic current, that had so strongly moved him. A moment, and he had caught it again; and with it this time came recollection in fullest flood.

Home! That was what they meant, those caressing appeals, those soft touches wafted through the air, those invisible little hands pulling and tugging, all one way!

Kenneth Grahame,
Wind in the Willows, 1908

RUNNING into the marsh among the familiar scents of roots, marsh plants, and slime and the extraneous smell of horse dung, Laska detected at once a smell that pervaded the whole marsh, the scent of that strong-smelling bird that always excited her more than any other. Here and there among the moss and marsh plants this scent was very strong, but it was impossible to determine in which direction it grew stronger or fainter. To find the direction, she had to go further away from the wind. Not feeling the motion of her legs, Laska bounded with a stiff gallop... Sniffing in the air with dilated nostrils, she felt at once that not their tracks only but they themselves were here before her, and not one, but many. Laska slackened her speed. They were here, but where precisely she could not yet determine. To find the very spot, she began to make a circle... The scent of them reached her, stronger and stronger, and more and more defined, and all at once it became perfectly clear to her that one of them was here, behind this tuft of reeds, five paces in front of her; she stopped, and her whole body was still and rigid. On her short legs she could see nothing in front of her, but by the scent she knew it was sitting not more than five paces off. She stood still, feeling more and more conscious of it, and enjoying it in anticipation. Her tail was stretched straight and tense, and only wagging at the extreme end. Her mouth was slightly open, her ears raised...

"Fetch it, fetch it!" shouted Levin, giving Laska a shove from behind.

Leo Tolstoy, Anna Karenina, 1877

ALTHOUGH the prey's sense of smell serves the hunter, his own odour can betray him; thus, he attempts to camouflage it beneath other scents. In Melanesia, the natives collect, dry, and preserve the nidorian glands of certain marsupials, which give off a strong, clinging odour. Before setting out on a hunt the men moisten the dried glands and rub them on their bodies, covering their human odour with the stronger, more feral scent, and the game, misled by this ploy, is then more easily approached. Melanesians also rub a salve on the bodies of young initiates that is designed to attract the "generosity" of the "guardian spirits of the hung." When the Ngbaka pygmies set out their traps in the forest, they first prepare themselves by acquiring a special smell. Bathing is avoided, as are clean garments. They rub their bodies with an odorous bark procured from the medicine man. Next they sprinkle their bodies with a special aromatic powder and fasten on a belt made of aromatic bark. The resulting complex odour, they believe, has the power to attract the forest spirits, or "Mimbo", who will in turn guide the game into the traps. Before returning to the village the hunters rid themselves of their dual-purpose odour, since it would be unbearable to others. They thrash their bodies with branches to release the forest spirits and make them return to their domain.

Annick Le Guérer, Scent, the Mysterious and
Essential Powers of Smell, 1993

DOGS can detect if someone has cancer just by sniffing the person's breath, a new study shows.

Ordinary household dogs with only a few weeks of basic "puppy training" learned to accurately distinguish between breath samples of lung- and breast-cancer patients and healthy subjects.

"Our study provides compelling evidence that cancers hidden beneath the skin can be detected simply by [dogs] examining the odors of a person's breath," said Michael McCulloch, who led the research.

Early detection of cancers greatly improves a patient's survival chances, and researchers hope that man's best friend, the dog, can become an important tool in early screening...

"Canine scent detection of cancer was something that was anecdotally discussed for decades, but we felt it was appropriate to design a rigorous study that seriously investigated this topic to better evaluate its effectiveness," said Nicholas Broffman, executive director of the Pine Street Foundation.

Cancer cells emit different metabolic waste products than normal cells," Broffman said. "The differences between these metabolic products are so great that they can be detected by a dog's keen sense of smell, even in the early stages of disease."

The researchers used a food reward-based method to train five ordinary household dogs.

By scent alone, the canines identified 55 lung and 31 breast cancer patients from those of 83 healthy humans.

The results of the study showed that the dogs could detect breast cancer and lung cancer between 88 and 97 percent of the time.

The high degree of accuracy persisted even after results were adjusted to take into account whether the lung cancer patients were currently smokers.

"It did not seem to matter which dog it was or which stage cancer it was, in terms of our results," Broffman said.

Stefan Lovgren
for National Geographic News

THUS, as a rule, fishes will not touch a bait that is not fresh, neither are they all caught by one and the same bait, but they are severally caught by baits suited to their several likings, and these baits they distinguish by their sense of smell; and, by the way, some fishes are attracted by malodorous baits, as the saupe, for instance, is attracted by excrement. Again, a number of fishes live in caves; and accordingly fishermen, when they want to entice them out, smear the mouth of a cave with strong-smelling pickles, and the fish are soon attracted to the smell. And the eel is caught in a similar way; for the fisherman lays down an earthen pot that has held pickles, after inserting a "weel" in the neck thereof. As a general rule, fishes are especially attracted by savoury smells. For this reason, fishermen roast the fleshy parts of the cuttle-fish and use it as bait on account of its smell, for fish are peculiarly attracted by it; they also bake the octopus and bait their fish-baskets or weels with it, entirely, as they say, on account of its smell. Furthermore, gregarious fishes, if fish washings or bilge-water be thrown overboard, are observed to scud off to a distance, from apparent dislike of the smell. And it is asserted that they can at once detect by smell the presence of their own blood; and this faculty is manifested by their hurrying off to a great distance whenever fish-blood is spilt in the sea. And, as a general rule, if you bait your weel with a stinking bait, the fish refuse to enter the weel or even to draw near; but if you bait the weel with a fresh and savoury bait, they come at once from long distances and swim into it. And all this is particularly manifest in the dolphin; for, as was stated, it has no visible organ of hearing, and yet it is captured when stupefied with noise; and so, while it has no visible organ for smell, it has the sense of smell remarkably keen.

Aristotle, The History of Animals, c383 BC

A cat's regard for his person is acutely traceable to a memory of life in the forest and plain. A cat does not chase his prey as a dog does; he can run swiftly for a short distance, but running is not his specialty. He lies in wait for his quarry and pounces upon it suddenly. Now some of the animals of which the cat is most fond for food, notably the mouse, have a keener sense of smell than their enemy; it is therefore essential for the good mouser to be devoid of odour. Consequently he washes and rewashes his fur and trims his whiskers to the last speck. "The love of dress is very marked in this attractive animal," writes Champfleury, "He is proud of the lustre of his coat, and cannot endure that a hair of it shall lie the wrong way. When the cat has eaten, he passes his tongue several times over both sides of his jaws, and his whiskers, in order to clean them thoroughly."

Carl Van Vechten,
The Tiger in the House, 1920

THEY say that the Leopard has a marvellous fragrance about it. To us it is imperceptible, though the Leopard is aware of the advantage it possesses, and other animals besides share with it this knowledge, and the Leopard catches them in the following manner. When the Leopard needs food it conceals itself in a dense thicket or in deep foliage and is invisible; it only breathes. And so fawns and gazelles and wild goats and suchlike animals are drawn by the spell, as it were, of its fragrance and come close up. Whereat the Leopard springs out and seizes its prey.

Claudius Aelianus, On the
Characteristics of Animals, c200

WHEN I think of dogs, I think of the smell of dog breath in the tight confines of the backseat of the family station wagon and the scent of fresh urine in the plush carpet; I think of the slippery feeling of saliva on my hands after a dog licks it; I think of the unsettling sensation of slipping and sliding barefoot on dog poop hidden in the freshly cut grass... I have trouble seeing past the body of the farting, panting, drooling, barking, shitting beast and into the spirit, the romantic ideal, of the domesticated pet. I find the myth of the dog fascinating, but the reality disgusting. Across twenty years of American television, nobody ever stepped in Lassie's poop.

Marsha Kinder,
Kid's Media Culture, 2000

WHY is it that no living creature except the panther has a pleasant smell? (The panther is pleasant even to beasts; for they say that other beasts enjoy sniffing it), and when they decompose they are also unpleasant, whereas many flowers, when they decay and wither, become more pleasantly scented?

Aristotle, Problems, c340BC

WITH some animals, as with the notorious skunk of America, the overwhelming odour which they emit appears to serve exclusively as a defence. With shrew-mice (Sorex) both sexes possess abdominal scent-glands and there can be little doubt, from the rejection of their bodies by birds and beasts of prey, that the odour is protective; nevertheless, the glands become enlarged in the males during the breeding-season. In many other quadrupeds the glands are of the same size in both sexes, but their uses are not known. In other species the glands are confined to the males, or are more developed than in the females; and they almost always become more active during the rutting-season. At this period the glands on the sides of the face of the male elephant enlarge, and emit a secretion having a strong musky odour. The males, and rarely the females, of many kinds of bats have glands and protrudable sacks situated in various parts; and it is believed that these are odoriferous....

In most cases, when only the male emits a strong odour during the breeding-season, it probably serves to excite or allure the female. We must not judge on this head by our own taste, for it is well known that rats are enticed by certain essential oils, and cats by valerian, substances far from agreeable to us; and that dogs, though they will not eat carrion, sniff and roll on it. From the reasons given when discussing the voice of the stag, we may reject the idea that the odour serves to bring the females from a distance to the males. Active and long-continued use cannot here have come into play, as in the case of the vocal organs. The odour emitted must be of considerable importance to the male, inasmuch as large and complex glands, furnished with muscles for everting the sack, and for closing or opening the orifice, have in some cases been developed. The development of these organs is intelligible through sexual selection, if the most odoriferous males are the most successful in winning the females, and in leaving offspring to inherit their gradually perfected glands and odours.

Charles Darwin, The Descent of Man
and Selection in Relation to Sex, 1871

POLECAT, polecat,
    Whatever made you smell like that?
You would really smell quite nice
Using aftershave Old Spice.

Spike Milligan, Polecat, 1991

ABOUT three miles beyond that, we passed over Stony creek, where one of those that guarded the baggage killed a polecat, upon which he made a comfortable repast. Those of his company were so squeamish they could not be persuaded at first to taste, as they said, of so unsavoury an animal; but seeing the man smack his lips with more pleasure than usual, they ventured at last to be of his mess, and instead of finding the flesh rank and high-tasted, they owned it to be the sweetest morsel they had ever eaten in their lives. The ill savour of this little beast lies altogether in its urine, which nature has made so detestably ill-scented on purpose to furnish a helpless creature with something to defend itself. For as some brutes have horns and hoofs, and others are armed with claws, teeth and tusks for their defence; and as some spit a sort of poison at their adversaries, like the paco; and others dart quills at their pursuers, like the porcupine; and as some have no weapons to help themselves but their tongues, and others none but their tails; so the poor polecat's safety lies altogether in the irresistible stench of its water; insomuch that when it finds itself in danger from an enemy, it moistens its bushy tail plentifully with this liquid ammunition, and then, with great fury, sprinkles it like a shower of rain full into the eyes of its assailant, by which it gains time to make its escape. Nor is the polecat the only animal that defends itself by a stink. At the cape of Good Hope is a little beast, called a stinker, as big as a fox, and shaped like a ferret, which being pursued has no way to save itself but by ejecting its wind and excrements, and then such a stench ensues that none of its pursuers can possibly stand it.

William Byrd, The Westover Manuscripts:
Containing the History of the Dividing Line betwixt Virginia and
Noth Carolina, c1733

NOW when Jimmy Skunk is angry, he doesn't bite and he doesn't scratch. You know Old Mother Nature has provided him with a little bag of perfume which Jimmy doesn't object to in the least, but which makes most people want to hold their noses and run. He never uses it, excepting when he is angry or in danger, but when he does use it, his enemies always turn tail and run. That is why he is afraid of no one, and why every one respects Jimmy and his rights.

Thornton W. Burgess,
The Adventures of Jimmy Skunk, 1994

THE African hunter Cumming tells us that the skin of the eland, as well as that of most other antelopes just killed, emits the most delicious perfume of trees and grass. I would have every man so much like a wild antelope, so much a part and parcel of Nature, that his very person should thus sweetly advertise our senses of his presence, and remind us of those parts of Nature which he most haunts. I feel no disposition to be satirical, when the trapper's coat emits the odour of musquash even; it is a sweeter scent to me than that which commonly exhales from the merchant's or the scholar's garments. When I go into their wardrobes and handle their vestments, I am reminded of no grassy plains and flowery meads which they have frequented, but of dusty merchants' exchanges and libraries rather.

Henry David Thoreau, *Walking, 1862*

THE most curious fact with respect to this animal, is the overpoweringly strong and offensive odour which proceeds from the buck. It is quite indescribable: several times whilst skinning the specimen which is now mounted at the Zoological Museum, I was almost overcome by nausea. I tied up the skin in a silk pocket-handkerchief, and so carried it home: this handkerchief, after being well washed, I continually used, and it was of course as repeatedly washed; yet every time, for a space of one year and seven months, when first unfolded, I distinctly perceived the odour. This appears an astonishing instance of the permanence of some matter, which nevertheless in its nature must be most subtile and volatile. Frequently, when passing at the distance of half a mile to leeward of a herd, I have perceived the whole air tainted with the effluvium. I believe the smell from the buck is most powerful at the period when its horns are perfect, or free from the hairy skin. When in this state the meat is, of course, quite uneatable; but the Gauchos assert, that if buried for some time in fresh earth, the taint is removed. I have somewhere read that the islanders in the north of Scotland treat the rank carcasses of the fish-eating birds in the same manner.

Charles Darwin, The Voyage of the Beagle, 1839

THOSE who have never seen, or rather smelled, a skunk can form no idea of the power of the perfume. The smell is quite unique, but has a flavour of onions about it, but its pungency nothing can describe.

I have myself seen dogs after attacking one go away coughing and gasping for breath; in fact, it has to be a mighty good dog to tackle one… The only way to get rid of the smell from clothing, etc, it so bury it; water is no good at all. There is a little story of the skunk as follows: – Sambo (a slave) had been whipped for stealing his master's onions. One day he appeared with a skunk in his arms. "Massa," said he, "here's de chap what steal de onions! Whew! Smell him bref!"

Percy G. Ebbutt, Emigrant Life in Kansas, 2004

THIS palace, where his siege is, is both great and passing fair. And within the palace, in the hall, there be twenty-four pillars of fine gold. And all the walls be covered within of red skins of beasts that men clepe panthers, that be fair beasts and well smelling; so that for the sweet odour of those skins no evil air may enter into the palace. Those skins be as red as blood, and they shine so bright against the sun, that unnethe no man may behold them. And many folk worship those beasts, when they meet them first at morning, for their great virtue and for the good smell that they have. And those skins they prize more than though they were plate of fine gold.

John Mandeville,
The Travels of Sir John Mandeville, 1357-1371

THE goddess fetched me up four seal skins from the bottom of the sea, all of them just skinned, for she meant to be playing a trick upon her father. Then she dug four pits for us to lie in, and sat down to wait till we should come up. When we were close to her, she made us lie down in the pits one after the other, and threw a seal skin over each of us. Our ambuscade would have been intolerable, for the stench of the fishy seals was most distressing – who would go to bed with a sea monster if he could help it? – but here, too, the goddess helped us, and thought of something that gave us great relief, for she put some ambrosia under each man's nostrils, which was so fragrant that it killed the smell of the seals.

Homer, The Odyssey, c700 BC

THE air is good to inhale in these valleys. And, if it is very warm, the dust bears with it a light odour of vanilla and of the stable, for so many cows pass over these routes that they leave reminders everywhere. And this odour is a perfume, when it would be a stench if it came from other animals.

Guy de Maupassant,
My Twenty-Five Days, 1885

CHAPTER V

*"Thy breasts shall be
as clusters of the vine,
and the smell of thy nose
like apples"*

The Odour of Sex and Death

OF lovers whose bodies smell of each other
    Who think the same thoughts without need of speech
And babble the same speech without need of meaning.

No peevish winter wind shall chill
No sullen tropic sun shall wither
The roses in the rose-garden which is ours and ours only.

T.S. Eliot, A Dedication to My Wife, 1958

the coming of my love emits
a wonderful smell in my mind,

you should see when i turn to find
her how my least heart-beat becomes less.

E. E. Cummings, when my love comes to see me,
Tulips and Chimneys, 1922

YOU forget that love is nothing but sweat, secretions, rancor.
    A simple matter of perspiration that begins in a nervous
moment called coup de foudre, continues between sour-smelling
sheets, and in the long run can only conclude in the proximity
of two bad moods by day and two bad smells at night, until the
final bankruptcy, the last lather, which is worked up by the fear
of no longer having anyone to sweat with. The question isn't, Is
the smell of love a stench or a perfume? but, What can be done to
make love, which essentially stinks, smell sweeter? What can be
done to banish the odor of betrayal, pettiness and falsehood that
sticks to the soles of lovers' shoes just when they think they are
walking on a bed of roses?

Linda Le, Slander, 1996

L ET him kiss me with the kisses of his mouth: for thy love is better than wine.

Because of the savour of thy good ointments thy name is as ointment poured forth, therefore do the virgins love thee.

...

While the king sitteth at his table, my spikenard sendeth forth the smell thereof.

A bundle of myrrh is my wellbeloved unto me; he shall lie all night betwixt my breasts.

My beloved is unto me as a cluster of camphire in the vineyards of En-gedi.

...

The flowers appear on the earth; the time of the singing of birds is come, and the voice of the turtle is heard in our land;

The fig tree putteth forth her green figs, and the vines with the tender grape give a good smell. Arise, my love, my fair one, and come away.

O my dove, that art in the clefts of the rock, in the secret places of the stairs, let me see thy countenance, let me hear thy voice; for sweet is thy voice, and thy countenance is comely.

...

Thy two breasts are like two young roes that are twins, which feed among the lilies.

Until the day break, and the shadows flee away, I will get me to the mountain of myrrh, and to the hill of frankincense.

Thou art all fair, my love; there is no spot in thee.

...

Thy lips, O my spouse, drop as the honeycomb: honey and milk are under thy tongue; and the smell of thy garments is like the smell of Lebanon.

...

I rose up to open to my beloved; and my hands dropped with myrrh, and my fingers with sweet smelling myrrh, upon the handles of the lock.

...

His cheeks are as a bed of spices, as sweet flowers: his lips like lilies, dropping sweet smelling myrrh.

...

I said, I will go up to the palm tree, I will take hold of the boughs thereof: now also thy breasts shall be as clusters of the vine, and the smell of thy nose like apples.

Song of Solomon,
King James Version of the Bible, 1611

THREE miles long and two streets wide, the town curls around the bay ... a gaudy run with Mediterranean splashes of color, crowded steep-pitched roofs, fishing piers and fishing boats whose stench of mackerel and gasoline is as aphrodisiac to the sensuous nose as the clean bar-whisky smell of a nightclub where call girls congregate.

Norman Mailer,
Advertisements for Myself on the Way Out, 1959

THE smells of the humours proved particularly amenable to interpretation. Barruel distinguished between male and female blood by odour. According to Bordeu, menstrual products emitted a specific smell that enabled mothers to watch over their daughters' physiology because "there is a large quantity of invisible emanations in menstrual excretion."... the decisive role was played by sperm, a "typical" liquid on which all the other humours were modelled. Semen by definition formed the essence of life. It exercised its effect on the totality of the organism; its odour betokened the individual's animality. According to Withof, the seminal humour "nurtured" the male organs and stimulated all the fibers; it produced "that fetid odour which vigorous males exude" and which eunuchs lacked. In man, this aura seminalis ensured the link, formed the connection between body and soul. The "unsubtle" odour of the pubescent male, arising from the discharge or flowback of semen into the blood and organs, should not, it was maintained, cause disgust.

Alain Corbin,
The Foul and the Fragrant, 1986

PHEROMONES are the pack animals of desire (from Greek, pherein, to carry, and horman, excite). Animals, like us, not only have distinctive odours, they also have powerfully effective pheromones, which trigger other animals into ovulation and courtship, or establish hierarchies of influence and power.

Diane Ackerman,
A Natural History of the Senses, 1990

STUDIES on mice conducted thirty or more years ago reveal that normal mating and reproduction are dependent upon the presence of a fully functional nose. Female mice surgically deprived of their olfactory bulbs showed a marked regression of their ovaries and uteri. Such mice never come on heat and the part of the ovary that would support the earliest phase of pregnancy – the corpus luteum – were small and undeveloped. Males similarly treated had altered seminal fluid, though sperm production was unaffected. Further work showed that if normal, pregnant female mice were exposed to the odour of males of a different strain, their embryos would be resorbed and they would come back on heat once more. The odour of the urine of an unfamiliar male, or of his bedding, was sufficient to block the females' pregnancy. Such experiments have not, of course, been carried out on humans but physicians have long reported the existence of some sort of connection between the nose and human reproduction. Nasal congestion often accompanies menstruation and pregnancy, and nosebleeds are a regular accompaniment of puberty in both sexes and sometimes of sexual excitement. As long ago as 1856 a Spanish physician noted abnormalities to, or even absence altogether or the olfactory bulbs in men with severe testicular regression. Modern research is revealing that malformation of the olfactory area of the brain is often associated with failure of sexual maturation to occur, or only a partial completion of it.

Michael Stoddart, The Scented Ape, 1990

A MONG far-flung tribes in a number of countries – Bourneo, on the Gambia River in West Africa, in Burma, in Siberia, in India – the word for "kiss" means "smell"; a kiss is really a prolonged smelling of one's beloved, relative, or friend. Members of a tribe in New Guinea say goodbye by putting a hand in each other's armpit, withdrawing it and stroking it over themselves, thus becoming coated with the friend's scent; other cultures sniff each other or rub noses in greeting.

Diane Ackerman,
A Natural History of the Senses, 1990

I N 1572 was celebrated the marriage of the King of Navarre with Margaret of Valois, at the Louvre, and that of the Prince of Condé with Mary of Cleves, endowed with singular beauty and goodness, and aged only 16. After having danced a long time, and finding herself somewhat incommoded by the heat of the ball, this princess passed into a cloakroom where one of the chambermaids of the Queen Mother caused her to change her chemise. She was about to issue when the Duc d'Anjou (Henri III) entered there in order to brush his hair, and by mistake wiped his face with the chemise she came to leave. From that moment the prince conceived for her the most violent passion.

Charles Féré, L'Instinct Sexuel, 1899

P REISMAN in 1877 makes the statement that for six hours after coitus there is a peculiar odor noticeable in the breath, owing to a peculiar secretion of the buccal glands. He says that this odor is most perceptible in men of about thirty-five, and can be discerned at a distance of from four to six feet. He also adds that this act would be of great medicolegal value in the early arrest of those charged with rape. In this connection the analogy of the breath after coitus to the odor of chloroform has been mentioned. The same article states that after coitus naturally foul breath becomes sweet.

Gould and Pyle,
Anomalies and Curiosities of Medicine, 1897

J'ARRIVE. Ne te lave pas.

[I'm coming home. Don't wash.]

> Dispatch from Napoleon to Josephine
> during his Italian Campaign: c1797

I am driving to you and I will drive all the way to New York / through the long round of the earth the plains / the wheat / through the hills of Ohio and the darkening cities of Pittsburgh and Philadelphia and Trenton / don't wash / I am listening to music loud / I can't stop / I am driving right into you with my foot my heart my fist / the faster I go the closer I am to you / I only slow down for police cars hidden behind the corners of the highway / behind well-placed trees and planned hillocks / I won the last battle / I won in all my short and skinny frame / at least 1500 hearts / because of you they saw me / because of you they saw what I have to offer / they cried in ecstacy when I tore off their clothes / they cried when I sliced open their throats / they cried when they saw everything I can give you / they wanted my hardness the curl of my lip / they wanted the murderer in me / don't wash / I want a week's worth of you wet / I want the same underwear the same sour smell / layers of it thick / the soak and musk of you / I too am acquiring mud and the scum of desire / my cock has not come down yet from thinking about you / through the entire days of battle don't wash / it's becoming night now / I see pinks and blue a deer by the side of the road / I'm driving south now into the constant drench of you the earth on my left shoulder / don't wash don't wash the books out of your hands / don't wash the telephone you've held between your chin and my mouth / don't wash away the meal you had this morning the orange juice on your chin / don't wash the history of the breaths you have taken in my absence out of your mouth / I want to know them / all the churches and all the stores smell me as I go by / they smell my desire and the force of my lips / they smell how I hold my breath the inside of your shoes / that white layer now at the fold where your thigh touches your labia that punk / your hair matted waiting / wait that long that much / I want you not to move and therefore not to live except to feel the force of my hand on your forehead / around your jaw / taste my mouth / yellow lines / white lines / a horse in the road / I am not tired / I will drive through the night / I will not eat / the dirt still caked around my fingernails / this is what they want all of them / they smell what happens with you / that I a woman / have something to offer a woman that I have something to take her with / do not wash / you will crawl over me / with the mud of your days / with all the slime and smell and wild leaves of them / and I will fill myself on the sourness of your ass and your cunt as they ride between my thumb and forefinger / I will lick you clean / all of that will be mine / I have fasted for days waiting

Linda Smukler,
Home in Three Days, Don't Wash, 1996

WHEN I go down on a woman, I always hope that I can smell and taste her, and not her soap. The pussy has a divine natural fragrance that shouldn't be washed away or masked with deodorant spray. The smell of a woman's arousal is intoxicating. Whoever said that pussy smells like tuna fish is a fucking idiot. I won't touch a tuna fish sandwich with a ten foot pole, but if someone could find a way to bottle the scent of a woman, I'd buy it and splash some on everyday. Right after my shower even.

http://www.lippyimp.com/smell.htm

NEVERTHELESS, some windfalls came in their way now and then in the shape of louis picked up in the society of elegant gentlemen, who slipped their decorations into their pockets as they went upstairs with them. Satin had an especially keen scent for these. On rainy evenings, when the dripping city exhaled an unpleasant odour suggestive of a great untidy bed, she knew that the soft weather and the fetid reek of the town's holes and corners were sure to send the men mad. And so she watched the best dressed among them, for she knew by their pale eyes what their state was. On such nights it was as though a fit of fleshly madness were passing over Paris.

Emile Zola, Nana, 1889

AS soon as Swann, on taking the Marquise's hand, had seen her bosom at close range and from above, he plunged an attentive, serious, absorbed, almost anxious gaze into the depths of her corsage, and his nostrils, drugged by her perfume, quivered like the wings of a butterfly about to alight upon a half-glimpsed flower

Marcel Proust, Sodom and Gomorrah, 1921

PSYCHO-ANALYSIS has cleared up one of the remaining gaps in our understanding of fetishism. It has shown the importance, as regards the choice of fetish, of a coprophilic pleasure in smelling which has disappeared owing to repression. Both the feet and the hair are objects with a strong smell which have been exalted into fetishes after the olfactory sensation has become unpleasurable and been abandoned. Accordingly, in the perversion that corresponds to foot-fetishism, it is only dirty and evil-smelling feet that become sexual objects.

Sigmund Freud,
Fixations of Preliminary Sexual Aims, 1910

August 9th

I'LL take another look at your slippers again... I think I love them as much as I do you.... I breathe their perfume, they smell of verbena – and of you in a way that makes my heart swell.

August 13th

YOUR mitten is here. It smells sweet, making me feel that I am still breathing the perfume of your shoulder and the sweet warmth of your bare arms.

August 15th

TELL me if you use verbena; do you not put it on your handkerchiefs? Put some on your slip. But no – do not use perfume, the best perfume is yourself, your own fragrance.

Gustav Flaubert, letters to Louise Colet, 1846

and this day it was Spring.... us
drew lewdly the murmurous minute clumsy
smelloftheworld. We intricately
alive, cleaving the luminous stammer of bodies
(eagerly just not each other touch)seeking, some
street which easily trickles a brittle fuss
of fragile huge humanity....

E. E. Cummings, and this day it was Spring, 1925

LE PARFUM

L ECTEUR, as-tu quelquefois respiré
Avec ivresse et lente gourmandise
Ce grain d'encens qui remplit une église,
Ou d'un sachet le musc invétéré?

Charme profond, magique, don't nous grise
Dans le présent le passé restauré!
Ainsi l'amant sur un corps adoré
Du souvenir cueille la fleur exquise.

De ses cheveux élastiques le lourds,
Vivant sachet, encensoir de l'alcôve,
Un senteur montait, sauvage et fauve,

Et des habits, mousseline ou velours,
Tout imprégnés de sa jeunesse pure,
Se dégageiat un parfum de fourrure.

[Reader, have you sometimes breathed in, with intoxication and slow greediness, the grain of incense which fills a church or the persistent musk of a sachet?

Profound, magical spell which captures us when, in the present, the past is restored! Even so the lover from an adored body plucks memory's exquisite flower.

From her elastic, heavy hair, a living sachet, thurible of the alcove, a smell arose, savage and wild,

And from the clothes, muslin or velvet, all impregnated with her pure youthfulness, there emanated a scent of fur.]

Charles Baudelaire, Le Parfum, 1857

DURING an exercise two weeks ago, marking the end of a specialized workshop for non-commissioned rescue officers, bottles containing the "smell of dead bodies" were scattered around the simulated "disaster site" to provide a feeling of real-life disaster...

The search for a scent resembling the dead was not an easy task. Rescue and medical professionals, who are familiar with the stench from personal experience, tested several chemical and organic substances before finding the exact "smell of death"...

"The strong smell is a significant part of every rescue incident," [Army commander Yisrael] Rozin said. "It's important that our soldiers, who will have to handle situations like this in the future, adapt to a situation as close to reality as possible, to prevent shock during the moment of truth."

Ynetnews.com, Israeli newspaper, 2005

WRITERS talk about the sweet-sick smell of death whereas any junky can tell you that death has no smell...at the same time a smell that shuts off breath and stops blood...colorless no-smell of death...no one can breathe and smell it through pink convolutions and black blood filters of flesh...the death smell is unmistakably a smell and complete absence of smell...smell absence hits the nose first because all organic life has smell... stopping of smell is felt like darkness to the eyes, silence to the ears, stress and weightlessness to the balance and location sense.

William S. Burroughs, Naked Lunch, 1959

TO the one a stench from death to death; to the other a sweet aroma from life to life. Who is sufficient for these things?

2 Corinthians, 2: 16, World English Bible, c2002

"HE smelt of death.".…

"But what does it smell like?" Fernando asked. "What odor has it? If there be an odor it must be a definite odor.".…

"Part of it is the smell that comes when, on a ship, there is a storm and the portholes are closed up. Put your nose against the brass handle of a screwed-tight porthole on a rolling ship that is swaying under you so that you are faint and hollow in the stomach and you have a part of that smell… After that of the ship you must go down the hill in Madrid to the Puente de Toledo early in the morning to the matadero … and wait for the old women who go before daylight to drink the blood of the beasts that are slaughtered… Kiss one, Inglés, for thy knolwedge's sake and then, with this in thy nostrils, walk back up into the city and when thou seest a refuse pail with dead flowers in it plunge thy nose deep into it and inhale so that scent mixes with those thou hast already in thy nasal passages … it is important that the day be in autumn with rain, or at least some fog, or early winter even and now thou shouldst continue to walk through the city and down the Calle de Salud smelling what thou wilt smell where they are sweeping out the casas de putas and emptying the slop jars into the drains and, with this odor of love's labor lost mixed sweetly with soapy water and cigarette butts only faintly reaching thy nostrils, thou shouldst … find an abandoned gunny sack with the odor of the wet earth, the dead flowers, and the doings of that night. In this sack will be contained the essence of it all, both the dead earth and the dead stalks of the flowers and their rotted blooms and the smell that is both the death and birth of man.

Ernest Hemingway, For Whom the Bell Tolls, 1940

THE brig came on slowly, and now more steadily than before, and – I cannot speak calmly of this event – our hearts leaped up wildly within us, and we poured out our whole souls in shouts and thanksgiving to God for the complete, unexpected, and glorious deliverance that was so palpably at hand. Of a sudden, and all at once, there came wafted over the ocean from the strange vessel (which was now close upon us) a smell, a stench, such as the whole world has no name for – no conception of – hellish – utterly suffocating – insufferable, inconceivable. I gasped for breath, and turning to my companions, perceived that they were paler than marble. But we had now no time left for question or surmise – the brig was within fifty feet of us, and it seemed to be her intention to run under our counter, that we might board her without putting out a boat. We rushed aft, when, suddenly, a wide yaw threw her off full five or six points from the course she had been running, and, as she passed under our stern at the distance of about twenty feet, we had a full view of her decks. Shall I ever forget the triple horror of that spectacle? Twenty-five or thirty human bodies, among whom were several females, lay scattered about between the counter and the galley in the last and most loathsome state of putrefaction. We plainly saw that not a soul lived in that fated vessel!

Edgar Allan Poe, The Narrative of
Arthur Gordon Pym of Nantucket, 1850

COW and horse dung, as muck goes, are relatively agreeable. You can even become nostalgic about them. They smell of fermented grain, and on the far side of their smell there is hay and grass. Chicken shit is disagreeable and rasps the throat because of the quantity of ammonia. When you are cleaning out the henhouse, you're glad to go to the door and take a deep breath of fresh air. Pig and human excrement, however, smell the worst because men and pigs are carnivorous and their appetites are indiscriminate. The smell includes the sickeningly sweet one of decay. And on the far side of it is death.

John Berger, "Muck and Its Entanglements," Harper's, 1989

RETURNING to the jeep was one of the most horrible experiences of my life. Perhaps it was that the breeze shifted or died; I do not know. But I walked into a veritable lake of stench. There was not a body in sight; the bodies must have been dragged into the brush just off the road, but the hot sun was directly on them. I had smelled the sharp, sweet, gaseous odor of death before, but nothing like this. It inflamed the nostrils, and I could even taste it in my mouth. Each breath drew it in deeply. I began to choke, and water streamed from my eyes. I started to run blindly up the road, which made me breathe more heavily. All my insides were convulsed, and I felt vomit in my throat. I was almost in a fainting condition when I reached the jeep, and I stayed sick for hours afterwards. The sight of death is nothing like its smell.

Eric Sevareid, Not So Wild a Dream, 1946

WHILE your eyes are drinking in the characteristics of Bonny scenery you notice a peculiar smell – an intensification of that smell you noticed when nearing Bonny, in the evening, out at sea. That's the breath of the malarial mud, laden with fever, and the chances are you will be down tomorrow. If it is near evening time now, you can watch it becoming incarnate, creeping and crawling and gliding out from the side creeks and between the mangrove-roots, laying itself upon the river, stretching and rolling in a kind of grim play, and finally crawling up the side of the ship to come on board and leave its cloak of moisture that grows green mildew in a few hours over all. Noise you will not be much troubled with: there is only that rain, a sound I have known make men who are sick with fever well-nigh mad, and now and again the depressing cry of the curlews which abound here. This combination is such that after six or eight hours of it you will be thankful to hear your shipmates start to work the winch. I take it you are hard up when you relish a winch. And you will say – let your previous experience of the world be what it may – Good Heavens, what a place!

Mary Kingsley, Travels in West Africa, 1897

OFTEN he slept for only an hour and then would stay sitting, not thinking anything, his nose catching whatever whiffs of death wafted from the smallest thicket. Even the invasive eucalyptus that was capable of sucking up all the land's water could not impose its fresh scent. The pungent smell of human death was killing the smell of the trees... From the nine or ten buildings a stink arose that was more revolting than liquid pig manure freshly spread on a summer's day. It was not just the smell of death but of all deaths and all rotting things.

Gil Courtemanche, A Sunday at the
Pool in Kigali, 2003

NO, I defy all counsel, all redress,
But that which ends all counsel, true redress:
Death, death. O amiable lovely death!
Thou odouriferous stench! sound rottenness!
Arise forth from the couch of lasting night,
Thou hate and terror to prosperity,
And I will kiss thy detestable bones,
And put my eyeballs in thy vaulty brows,
And ring these fingers with thy household worms,
And stop this gap of breath with fulsome dust,
And be a carrion monster like thyself.

William Shakespeare, King John, 1598

BENEATH is all the fiends': there's hell, there's darkness,
There is the sulphurous pit, burning, scalding,
Stench, consumption. Fie, fie, fie! pah, pah!
Give me an ounce of civet; good apothecary,
Sweeten my imagination. There's money for thee.

William Shakespeare, King Lear, 1605

THERE was a damned successful Poet;
   There was a Woman like the Sun.
And they were dead. They did not know it.
They did not know their time was done.
They did not know his hymns
Were silence; and her limbs,
That had served Love so well,
Dust, and a filthy smell.

Rupert Brooke, Dead Man's Love, 1911

LITTLE Johann stood beside the bier among his black-clad relatives. He had a broad mourning band on his own sailor suit, and his senses felt misty with the scent from countless bouquets and wreaths – and with another odour that came wafted now and then on a current of air, and smelled strange, yet somehow familiar... This was not Grandmamma... Death had turned her for ever into this wax figure that kept is lids and lips so forbiddingly closed... He held his head on one side, the curly light-brown locks swaying over the temples, and looked with his gold-brown blue-encircled eyes in brooding repugnance upon the face of the dead. His breath came long and shuddering, for he kept expecting that strange, puzzling odour which all the scent of the flowers sometimes failed to disguise. When the odour came, and he perceived it, he drew his brows still more together, his lip trembled, and the long sigh which he gave was so like a tearless sob that Frau Permaneder bent over and kissed him and took him away.

Thomas Mann, Buddenbrooks, 1902

CASSANDRA
Pah!
CHORUS
What is this cry? some dark despair of soul?
CASSANDRA
Pah! the house fumes with stench and spilth of blood.
CHORUS
How? 'tis the smell of household offerings.
CASSANDRA
'Tis rank as charnel-scent from open graves.
CHORUS
Thou canst not mean this scented Syrian nard?
CASSANDRA
Nay, let me pass within to cry aloud
The monarch's fate and mine – enough of life.
Ah friends!
Bear to me witness, since I fall in death,
That not as birds that shun the bush and scream
I moan in idle terror. This attest
When for my death's revenge another dies,
A woman for a woman, and a man
Falls, for a man ill-wedded to his curse.
Grant me this boon – the last before I die.

Aeschylus, Agamemnon,
The Oresteia, 458BC

FIE on thee, said Corsabrin, do thy worst. Then he smote off his
head. And therewithal came a stink of his body when the soul
departed, that there might nobody abide the savour. So was the
corpse had away and buried in a wood, because he was a paynim.
Then they blew unto lodging, and Palomides was unarmed.

Thomas Malory,
Le Morte D'Arthur, 1485

THE idea held by the Greek philosophers such as Socrates that odours should reflect social classes had its origins in the religious notions of the times, which ascribed to the gods the very best odours imaginable. How this arose is not known but it may have been related to the sweetish odour which not infrequently accompanies death, perhaps caused by some preliminary tissue degeneration processes occurring. From this it would be easy to understand how the idea could develop that the soul requires fine odour to enable it to break clear from the body and start its ascent. Aztecs offered perfumed flowers on the graves of the departed daily for four years, as this was the time the spirit supposedly needed to reach heaven.

Michael Stoddart,
The Scented Ape, 1990

THE undertaker's men dug carefully, holding their shovel blades almost parallel to the ground and tossing aside little scoops of soil. They wore bandanas across their faces. Everyone else breathed through handkerchiefs. The smell was already as strong as a vision. There is no odor like the odor of a dead human. It's a saccharine putrescence – rotting meat and prom corsages, a sweet, gagging stink. It penetrates clothes and skin. No matter how many times you shower, no matter how many times you tell the poor laundry girl at the hotel to take your clothes back and wash them again, the scent returns like a worry or an evil thought. It's not even such a bad smell, no worse than whiskey vomit, but the reek of our own death goes like a shock to some early, unevolved ganglion just at the head of the spine, to the home of all wordless, thoughtless fear.

P.J. O'Rourke, *Holidays in Hell, 2000*

THERE were at La Fère some gentlemen charged to find the dead body of M. de Bois-Dauphin the elder, who had been killed in the battle; they asked me to go with them to the camp, to pick him out, if we could, among the dead; but it was not possible to recognize him, the bodies being all far gone in corruption, and their faces changed. We saw more than half a league round us the earth all covered with the dead; and hardly stopped there, because of the stench of the dead men and their horses; and so many blue and green flies rose from them, bred of the moisture of the bodies and the heat of the sun, that when they were up in the air they hid the sun. It was wonderful to hear them buzzing; and where they settled, there they infected the air, and brought the plague with them. Mon petit maistre, I wish you had been there with me, to experience the smells, and make report thereof to them that were not there.

Ambroise Paré, Battle of
Saint Quentin, 1557

"NOW, by my faith, sir," quoth Sancho, "I have already touched them, and find this devil that goeth there so busily up and down, both plump and soft-fleshed; and that he hath besides another property very different from that which I have heard say devils have; for it is said that they smell all of brimstone and other filthy things, but one may feel, at least half a league off, the amber that this devil smells of." Sancho spoke this of Don Fernando, who belike, as lords of his rank are wont, had his attire perfumed with amber.

"Marvel not thereat, friend Sancho," quoth Don Quixote; "for the devils are very crafty, and although they bring smells or perfumes about them, yet they themselves smell nothing, because they are spirits; or if they do smell aught, it is not good, but evil and stinking savours: the reason is, for that as they do always bear, wheresoever they be, their hell about them, and can receive no kind of ease of their torments, and good smells be things that delight and please, it is not possible that they can smell any good thing; and if it seem to thee that that devil whom thou dost mention smells of amber, either thou art deceived, or he would deceive thee, by making thee to think that he is no devil."

Miguel de Cervantes Saavedra , Don Quixote, 1605

"THIS is the spot," said the Professor as he turned his lamp on a small map of the house, copied from the file of my original correspondence regarding the purchase. With a little trouble we found the key on the bunch and opened the door. We were prepared for some unpleasantness, for as we were opening the door a faint, malodorous air seemed to exhale through the gaps, but none of us ever expected such an odour as we encountered. None of the others had met the Count at all at close quarters, and when I had seen him he was either in the fasting stage of his existence in his rooms or, when he was bloated with fresh blood, in a ruined building open to the air, but here the place was small and close, and the long disuse had made the air stagnant and foul. There was an earthy smell, as of some dry miasma, which came through the fouler air. But as to the odour itself, how shall I describe it? It was not alone that it was composed of all the ills of mortality and with the pungent, acrid smell of blood, but it seemed as though corruption had become itself corrupt. Faugh! It sickens me to think of it. Every breath exhaled by that monster seemed to have clung to the place and intensified its loathsomeness.

Under ordinary circumstances such a stench would have brought our enterprise to an end, but this was no ordinary case, and the high and terrible purpose in which we were involved gave us a strength which rose above merely physical considerations. After the involuntary shrinking consequent on the first nauseous whiff, we one and all set about our work as though that loathsome place were a garden of roses.

Bram Stoker, Dracula, 1897

MY flesh had not been long stripped off when she
had me descend through all the rings of Hell,
to draw a spirit back from Judas' circle.
That is the deepest and the darkest place,
the farthest from the heaven that girds all:
so rest assured, I know the pathway well.
This swamp that breeds and breathes the giant stench.

Dante Alighieri, Inferno, IX, c1312

ALONG the upper rim of a high bank
formed by a ring of massive broken boulders,
we came above a crowd more cruelly pent.
And here, because of the outrageous stench
thrown up in excess by that deep abyss,
we drew back till we were behind the lid
of a great tomb, on which I made out this,
inscribed: "I hold Pope Anastasius,
enticed to leave the true path by Photinus."
"It would be better to delay descent
so that our senses may grow somewhat used
to this foul stench; and then we can ignore it."

Dante Alighieri, Inferno, XI, c1312

CHAPTER VI

*"Stagnant water
and
dead cats"*

The Stench of History

IF we have largely forgotten the physical discomforts of the itching, oppressive garments of the past ... then we have mercifully forgotten, too, the smells of the past, the domestic odours – ill-washed flesh; infrequently changed underwear; chamber-pots; slop-pails; inadequately plumbed privies; rotting food; unattended teeth; and the streets are no fresher than indoors, the omnipresent acridity of horse piss and dung, drains, the sudden stench of old death from butchers' shops, the amniotic horror of the fishmonger.

Angela Carter,
The Fall River Axe Murders, 1981

IN America the sassafras is divided into two varieties, the red and white. Its great use is for medicinal purposes. It is however employed in America for making bedsteads and other articles of furniture, which are not liable to the attacks of insects, and give out a very agreeable odour. This plant is interesting in connection with the history of America, as it is said that it was its strong aromatic smell that convinced Columbus, when seeking the New World, that a shore was near at hand, and encouraged him to persevere, at a time when his crew had mutinied, and the failure of attaining the objects of his expedition was threatened.

George Long,
The Penny Cyclopaedia of the
Society for the Diffusion of Useful Knowledge, 1833

FLEET Market, at that time, was a long irregular row of wooden sheds and penthouses, occupying the centre of what is now called Farringdon Street. They were jumbled together in a most unsightly fashion, in the middle of the road; to the great obstruction of the thoroughfare and the annoyance of passengers, who were fain to make their way, as they best could, among carts, baskets, barrows, trucks, casks, bulks, and benches, and to jostle with porters, hucksters, waggoners, and a motley crowd of buyers, sellers, pick–pockets, vagrants, and idlers. The air was perfumed with the stench of rotten leaves and faded fruit; the refuse of the butchers' stalls, and offal and garbage of a hundred kinds. It was indispensable to most public conveniences in those days, that they should be public nuisances likewise; and Fleet Market maintained the principle to admiration.

Charles Dickens,
Barnaby Rudge, 1840

MR. Johnson and I walked arm-in-arm up the High-street, to my house in James's court: it was a dusky night: I could not prevent his being assailed by the evening effluvia of Edinburgh. I heard a late baronet, of some distinction in the political world in the beginning of the present reign, observe, that "walking the streets of Edinburgh at night was pretty perilous, and a good deal odoriferous." The peril is much abated, by the care which the magistrates have taken to enforce the city laws against throwing foul water from the windows; but, from the structure of the houses in the old town, which consist of many stories, in each of which a different family lives, and there being no covered sewers, the odour still continues. A zealous Scotsman would have wished Mr. Johnson to be without one of his five senses upon this occasion. As we marched slowly along, he grumbled in my ear, "I smell you in the dark!" But he acknowledged that the breadth of the street, and the loftiness of the buildings on each side, made a noble appearance.

James Boswell, Journal of a
Tour to the Hebrides, 1785

THEN, one week, later, when the tombs were consolidated and the house of the poor lady was demolished, I entered the tomb. When I entered the burial chamber, I saw a very large anthropoid sarcophagus. I will never forget that moment. The burial chamber was very small but a beautiful sarcophagus was found inside. At that moment of discovery, I felt as though arrows of fire were attacking me. My eyes were closed, and I could not breath [sic] because of bad smell [sic]. I looked into the room and discovered a very thick yellow powder around the anthropoid sarcophagus. I cold [sic] not walk and did not read the name of the owner. I ran back out because of this smell.

From journals of Dr Zahi A. Hawass
(General Director of the Giza Pyramid,
Saqqara and Baharia Oasis), 1999

HIS body, presently after his expiration, was washed and laid out; and being opened, was embalmed, and wrapped in a sere cloth six double, and put into an inner sheet of lead, inclosed in an elegant coffin of the choicest wood. Owing to the disease he died of, which, by the by, appeared to be that of poison, his body, although thus bound up and laid in the coffin, swelled and bursted, from whence came such filth, that raised such a deadly and noisome stink, that it was found prudent to bury him immediately, which was done in as private a manner as possible...

The corpse being thus quickly buried, by reason of the great stench thereof, a rich coffin of state was, on the 26th of September, about ten at night, privately removed from Whitehall, in a mourning hearse, attended by his domestic servants, to Somersethouse, in the Strand, where it remained in private for some days, till all things were prepared for public view; which being accomplished, the effigies of his Highness was, with great state and magnificence, exposed openly, multitudes daily crowding to see this glorious, but mournful sight.

Thomas Burton, Cromwell's Death and Funeral Order,
in Diary of Thomas Burton, esq, volume 2,

IF I am asked how anyone can stay in this filthy haunt of all the vice and all the diseases piled one on top of the other, amid an air poisoned by a thousand putrid vapours, among butchers' shops, cemeteries, hospitals, drains, streams of urine, heaps of excrement, dyers', tanners', curriers' stalls; in the midst of continual smoke from that unbelievable quantity of wood, and the vapour from all that coal; in the midst of the arsenic, bituminous, and sulphurous parts that are ceaselessly exhaled by workshops where copper and metal are wrought: if I am asked how anyone lives in this abyss, where the heavy, fetid air is so thick that it can be seen, and its atmosphere smelled, for three leagues around; air that cannot circulate, but only whirls around within this labyrinth of houses: finally, how man can willingly crawl into these prisons whereas he would see that, if he released the animals that he has bent to his yoke, their purely instinctive reaction would be to escape precipitously to the fields in search of air, greenness, a free soil perfumed by the scent of flowers: I would reply that familiarty accustoms the Parisians to humid fogs, maleficent vapours, and foul-smelling ooze.

Louis-Sébastien Mercier, Tableau de Paris, 1782-88

THUS, holding a bit of your massapa in your mouth, and holding the hand with the aforementioned fragrances under the nose and in the other the aforementioned branche of burning juniper, you must look upon your patient from a certain distance away and enquire into his sicknesse and his symptoms and whether he be in paine, or if he hath any tumor anywhere, and so converse with him. And then, approaching him, and with your backe turned upon him, you will hand your branche of wood to someone who will continue to hold it before your face and, reaching behind you with your hand, you will take the patient's pulse and feele his forehead and the region of his harte, always maintaining some fragrance beneath your nose.

Ogier Ferrier, Remèdes,
Préservatifs et Curatifs de Peste, 1548

THE unpleasant odours in the park, gardens, even the château, make one's gorge rise. The communicating passages, courtyards, buildings in the wings, corridors, are full of urine and faeces; a pork butcher actually sticks and roasts his pigs at the bottom of the ministers' wing every morning; the avenue Saint-Cloud is covered with stagnant water and dead cats.

La Morandière,
report on Versailles, 1764

THERE is a stench that is similar to the one exuded by clothes, and there is a moldy smell that is less noticeable but nevertheless more unpleasant because of the general revulsion it arouses. A third, which might be called the odour of decomposition, may be described as a mixture of the acidic, the sickly, and the fetid; it provokes nausea rather than offending the nose. This mixture accompanies decomposition and is the most repellent among all the odours to be encountered in a hospital. Another odour, which makes the nose and eyes burn, results from uncleanliness. It gives the impression that the air contains something like powder, and, if one looks for the source, one is certain to find damp mouldy laundry, a pile of rubbish or clothes and bedclothes infested by fermenting miasmas. Each infectious material has its distinctive exhalation. Doctors know the special smell of a septic wound, of a cancerous agent, and the pestilential odour that is spread by caries. But what physicians have learned of this subject from experience can be tested by anyone who compares the various odours in the wards. In the pediatric ward the smell is sour and stinking; in the women's wards it is sweet and putrid; the men's wards, on the other hand, exude a strong odour that merely stinks and hence is not so repulsive. Although there is now a greater emphasis on cleanliness than in earlier times, in the wards occupied by the good poor of Bicêtre there prevails a flat odour that produces an effect of nausea in delicate constitutions.

Jean-Noël Hallé, Air des hôpitaux
de terre et de mer, 1787

BETWEENE these two rehearsed extremities of life, there were other of a more moderate temper, not being so daintily dieted as the first, nor drinking so dissolutely as the second; but used all things sufficient for their appetites, and without shutting up themselves, walked abroad, some carrying sweete nosegayes of flowers in their hands; others odoriferous herbes, and others divers kinds of spiceries, holding them to their noses, and thinking them most comfortable for the braine, because the ayre seemed to be much infected by the noysome smell of dead carkases, and other hurtfull savours. Some other there were also of more inhumane minde (howbeit peradventure it might be the surest) saying, that there was no better physicke against the pestilence, nor yet so good, as to flie away from it, which argument mainely moving them, and caring for no body but themselves, very many, both men and women, forsooke the City, their owne houses, their Parents, Kindred, Friends, and Goods, flying to other mens dwellings else-where.

Boccaccio, The Decameron, 1349-1352

THE food the most repugnant to sense or imagination, the aliments the most unwholesome and pernicious to the constitution, were eagerly devoured, and fiercely disputed, by the rage of hunger. A dark suspicion was entertained, that some desperate wretches fed on the bodies of their fellow-creatures, whom they had secretly murdered; and even mothers, (such was the horrid conflict of the two most powerful instincts implanted by nature in the human breast), even mothers are said to have tasted the flesh of their slaughtered infants! Many thousands of the inhabitants of Rome expired in their houses, or in the streets, for want of sustenance; and as the public sepulchres without the walls were in the power of the enemy the stench, which arose from so many putrid and unburied carcasses, infected the air; and the miseries of famine were succeeded and aggravated by the contagion of a pestilential disease.

*Edward Gibbon, The History of the Decline
and Fall of the Roman Empire, volume 2, 1781*

THIS immediately filled everybody's mouths with one preparation or another... so we perhaps as the physicians directed, in order to prevent infection by the breath of others; insomuch that if we came to go into a church, when it was anything full of people, there would be such a mixture of smells at the entrance, that if it was more strong, though perhaps not so unwholesome, than if you were going into an apothecary or druggist's shop; in a word, the whole church was like a smelling bottle, in one corner it was all perfumes, in another aromatics, balsamics and variety of drugs, and herbs; in another salts and spirits, as everyone furnished for their own preservation.

Daniel Defoe, The History
of the Great Plague, 1754

EACH quarter would specialize in a particular branch of business, all the artisans and traders of a single neighbourhood working at the same or at complementary crafts. Work in leather, for instance, was the speciality of the Argiletum and of its adjacent streets. In the Argiletum itself, books were manufactured and sold; nearby was the street of the sandal-makers, then the street of the tanners, permanently enveloped in the smell of the tannery. The stench of the Argiletum would accompany anyone on their way up to the Suburra, a quarter known for its low-life taverns and brothels. On the other side of the forum, dipping towards the Tiber, the street of the Tuscans boasted an array of luxury boutiques. There, where the smell of incense mingled with that of purple dyes stewing in stale urine, one might find beautiful papyrus scroll books and high-class prostitutes of both sexes. Each quarter had its own special smell, which its inhabitants no longer noticed but which would strike outsiders as a foul stench. The more sophisticated men, such as the praetor Verres, would seek to protect themselves with fragrant flowers when they went out on the town. Women and effeminate men would carry in their hands a ball of amber which from time to time they would rub and then sniff.

Florence Dupont, Daily Life in Ancient Rome, 1992

WALKED 6 miles before daylight and went in the trenches. They are filthy and horrible. Don't see how the men stand it. The stink of dead Huns in front is awful even in this cold weather. Soon after daylight I followed a party cleaning out an old communicating trench with hand grenades. I went on until I saw 4 boches killed by grenades and 2 bayoneted and 1 poilu shot through the head. It was sickening but I suppose I would get used to it. Everyone does. Late in afternoon the boches began shelling the trench and we retired to dugouts. I stood in the observation post a few minutes to see the show: but only until a shell landed near and the shock nearly knocked me over. I hunted the dugout also. One observer was wounded. After dark we started for the rear and I was relieved to get some pure air. After walking for miles in the cold I am writing this. The shells bursting at night are very pretty.

Marine Flyer in France,
The Diary of Captain Alfred A. Cunningham,
November 1917 - January 1918

DO you remember the dark months you held the sector at Mametz, –
The nights you watched and wired and dug and piled sandbags on parapets?
Do you remember the rats; and the stench
Of corpses rotting in front of the front-line trench, –
And dawn coming, dirty-white, and chill with a hopeless rain?
Do you ever stop and ask, "Is it all going to happen again?"

Siegfried Sassoon, Aftermath, 1919

WE were near the front line now, near enough to smell the characteristic smell of war – in my experience a smell of excrement and decaying food.

George Orwell, Homage to Catalonia, 1938

MOONLIGHT and dew-drenched blossom, and the scent
Of summer gardens; these can bring you all
Those dreams that in the starlit silence fall:
Sweet songs are full of odours.
                              While I went
Last night in drizzling dusk along a lane,
I passed a squalid farm; from byre and midden
Came the rank smell that brought me once again
A dream of war that in the past was hidden.

Siegfried Sassoon, The Dream, 1918

I sit in one of the dives
On Fifty-second Street
Uncertain and afraid
As the clever hopes expire
Of a low dishonest decade:
Waves of anger and fear
Circulate over the bright
And darkened lands of the earth,
Obsessing our private lives;
The Unmentionable odour of death
Offends the September night.

W.H. Auden, September 1, 1939, 1940

You smell that? Do you smell that? That's napalm, son! Nothing else in the world smells like that! I love the smell of napalm in the morning. You know, this one time, we bombed this hill, for twelve hours... When it was over I went up there... We didn't find one of 'em, not one stinkin' dink body. But, you know, that smell ... that gasoline smell... The whole hill... It smelled like ... victory.

Colonel Kilgore in Apocalypse Now, 1979

I was a broken wheel, a useless machine, with no companions and no food. I wandered to the place from which we started to charge, and there it was darkness and more lonely. Beyond I saw the glimmer of a light, and there I found the lady whom we had assisted. She bound up my hand, gave me water to drink and a kind word. I made my way back to the Chinn House, and lay down in the east portico. The house and yard were full of dead and wounded men, but fatigue, hunger and wretchedness were soon forgotten in welcome sleep. During the night a wounded captain was brought and laid down beside me, but when morning came he was a corpse.

A cold rain was falling, the surgeons were still busy amputating limbs, and the piles of legs and arms attested their patient work during the night. The sight was not calculated to cheer me. The smell of warm blood, in my exhausted condition, was too much for me, and for once I nearly fainted, but I went out into the cold rain and walked among the numerous dead, who covered the fields around.

W.R. Houghton and M.B Houghton,
Two Boys in the Civil War and After, 1912

FATHER Hamilton said that at one time the prisoners died at the rate of 150 a day, and he saw some of them die on the ground without a rag to lie on or a garment to cover them. Dysentery was the most fatal disease, and as they lay on the ground in their own excrements, the smell was so horrible that the good father says he was often obliged to rush from their presence to get a breath of pure air. It is dreadful. My heart aches for the poor wretches, Yankees though they are, and I am afraid God will suffer some terrible retribution to fall upon us for letting such things happen.

Eliza Frances Andrews, The War-Time
Journal of a Georgia Girl, 1864-1865

PRIOR to the Civil War the Capital was ruled, and the standards of its social and political life fixed, by an aristocracy founded on brains, culture, and blood. Power was with few exceptions intrusted to an honourable body of high-spirited public officials. Now a Negro electorate controlled the city government, and gangs of drunken negroes, its sovereign citizens, paraded the streets at night firing their muskets unchallenged and unmolested.

A new mob of onion-laden breath, mixed with perspiring African odour, became the symbol of American Democracy.

A new order of society sprouted in this corruption. The old high-bred ways, tastes, and enthusiasms were driven into the hiding-places of a few families and cherished as relics of the past.

Thomas Dixon, Jr., The Clansman, an
Historical Romance of the Ku Klux Klan, 1905

THE Nazi doesn't just emit the odour of blood – he gives off the reek of urine in a chamberpot as well – the stinking chamberpot of his morality, his horrors, his crimes, his ideology; he is a filthy, hell-hound of a beast... And to that smell of the blood of his past bestialities must be added the obscene odour of repression, the typically Nazi smell of stale, unaired bedclothes, a fitting accompaniment to the stench of urine.

Ernst Bloch, Le Temps de la peste,
mensurations politiques, le Vormärz, 1830-1848

IT was the beginning of May and a cool wind carried to us a peculiar, sweetish odour, much like that of burning flesh, although we did not identify it as that. The odour greeted us upon our arrival and stayed with us always...

Among the S.S. women, I knew Irma Griese best, not because of any personal wish, but because of circumstances beyond my control. The "blonde angel", as the press called her, inspired me to the most violent hatred I ever experienced...

This twenty-two-year-old S.S. was conscious of the power of her beauty and neglected nothing that would enhance its charms. She spent hours grooming herself before her mirror and practiced the most seductive gestures. Wherever she went she brought the scent of rare perfume. Her hair was sprayed with a complete range of tantalizing odours: sometimes she blended her own concoctions. Her immoderate use of perfume was perhaps the supreme refinement of her cruelty. The internees, who had fallen to a state of physical degradation, inhaled these fragrances joyfully. By contrast, when she left us and the stale, sickening odour of burnt human flesh, which covered the camp like a blanket, crept over us again, the atmosphere became even more unbearable. Yet our "angel" with the golden tresses employed her beauty only to remind us of her terrible position.

Olga Lengyel, Five Chimneys, 1947

THE ovens,
   the stench,
I couldn't repeat
the stench. You
have to breathe.
You can wipe out
what you don't want
to see. You don't want
to hear, don't want
to taste. You can
block out all senses
except smell.
...

And I went in
to take a picture
and the stench was so much
I couldn't.
...

A sour, putrid
smell that
left you ready
to throw up.

Barbara Helfott Hyett, In Evidence,
Poems of the Liberation of
Nazi Concentration Camps, 1986

CHAPTER VII

"The fragile,
    mucaceous
odor
    of Breakfast"

Food and Drink

AND beyond these isles there is another isle that is clept Pytan. The folk of that country ne till not, ne labour not the earth, for they eat no manner thing. And they be of good colour and of fair shape, after their greatness. But the small be as dwarfs, but not so little as be the Pigmies. These men live by the smell of wild apples. And when they go any far way, they bear the apples with them; for if they had lost the savour of the apples, they should die anon. They ne be not full reasonable, but they be simple and bestial.

John Mandeville,
The Travels of Sir John Mandeville, 1357-1371

TWICE a day, on his way to and from school, little Charlie Bucket had to walk right past the gates of the factory. And every time he went by, he would begin to walk very, very slowly, and he would hold his nose high in the air and take long deep sniffs of the gorgeous chocolatey smell all around him.

Oh, how he loved that smell!...

Sometimes he would stand motionless outside the gates for several minutes on end, taking deep swallowing breaths as though he were trying to eat the smell itself...

"How lovely and warm!" whispered Charlie.

"I know. And what a marvellous smell!" answered Grandpa Joe, taking a long deep sniff. All the most wonderful smells in the world seemed to be mixed up in the air around them – the smell of roasting coffee and burnt sugar and melting chocolate and mint and violets and crushed hazelnuts and apple blossom and caramel and lemon peel.

Roald Dahl,
Charlie and the Chocolate Factory, 1964

NOT long after the dram, may be expected the breakfast, a meal in which the Scots, whether of the lowlands or mountains, must be confessed to excel us. The tea and coffee are accompanied not only with butter, but with honey, conserves, and marmalades. If an epicure could remove by a wish, in quest of sensual gratifications, wherever he had supped he would breakfast in Scotland. In the Islands however, they do what I found it not very easy to endure. They pollute the tea-table by plates piled with large slices of cheshire cheese, which mingles its less grateful odours with the fragrance of the tea.

Samuel Johnson,
Journey to the Western Islands of Scotland, 1775

NOW there grows among all the rooms, replacing the night's old smoke, alcohol and sweat, the fragile, mucaceous odor of Breakfast: flowery, permeating, surprising, more than the color of winter sunlight, taking over not so much through any brute pungency or volume as by the high intricacy to the weaving of its molecules, sharing the conjuror's secret by which – though it is not often Death is told so clearly to fuck off – the living genetic chains prove even labyrinthine enough to preserve some human face down ten or twenty generations... so the same assertion-through-structure allows this war morning's banana fragrance to meander, repossess, prevail. Is there any reason not to open every window, and let the kind scent blanket all Chelsea?

Thomas Pynchon, Gravity's Rainbow, 1973

I love bread-and-butter pudding. I love its layers of sweet, quivering custard, juicy raisins, and puffed, golden crust. I love the way it sings quietly in the oven; the way it wobbles on the spoon.

You can't smell a hug. You can't hear a cuddle. But if you could, I reckon it would smell and sound of warm bread-and-butter pudding.

Nigel Slater, Toast, 2003

WHEN the girl returned, some hours later, she carried a tray, with a cup of fragrant tea steaming on it; and a plate piled up with very hot buttered toast, cut thick, very brown on both sides, with the butter running through the holes in it in great golden drops, like honey from the honeycomb. The smell of that buttered toast simply talked to Toad, and with no uncertain voice; talked of warm kitchens, of breakfasts on bright frosty mornings, of cosy parlour firesides on winter evenings, when one's ramble was over and slippered feet were propped on the fender; of the purring of contented cats, and the twitter of sleepy canaries. Toad sat up on end once more, dried his eyes, sipped his tea and munched his toast, and soon began talking freely about himself, and the house he lived in, and his doings there, and how important he was, and what a lot his friends thought of him.

...

A fire of sticks was burning near by, and over the fire hung an iron pot, and out of that pot came forth bubblings and gurglings, and a vague suggestive steaminess. Also smells – warm, rich, and varied smells – that twined and twisted and wreathed themselves at last into one complete, voluptuous, perfect smell that seemed like the very soul of Nature taking form and appearing to her children, a true Goddess, a mother of solace and comfort. Toad now knew well that he had not been really hungry before. What he had felt earlier in the day had been a mere trifling qualm. This was the real thing at last, and no mistake; and it would have to be dealt with speedily, too, or there would be trouble for somebody or something. He looked the gipsy over carefully, wondering vaguely whether it would be easier to fight him or cajole him. So there he sat, and sniffed and sniffed, and looked at the gipsy; and the gipsy sat and smoked, and looked at him.

Kenneth Grahame,
Wind in the Willows, 1908

THERE is no one in the world like the Parisian for eating what revolts the sense of smell.

Louis-Sébastien Mercier, Tableau de Paris, 1782-88

ONLY once have I eaten [at McDonald's]. It was interesting. I ate French fried potatoes, of course, and the kids ate a Big Mac. They tasted marvelous at first. Hot, wonderful smells. Halfway home they said, "We can't finish these now, we'll finish them at home." Four miles from home the car stank of this strange, cold, dead, bad oil. The girls opened the windows. Without mentioning it they dumped all this stuff in the garbage pail.

If you're starved or a truck driver, they taste very good. That was our experience with McDonald's.

*M.F.K. Fisher in conversation
with Joan Nathan, The Washington Post, 1986*

FROM the kitchen rose the smell of hot fish and crayfish soup. I felt that this smell was tickling my palate and nostrils, that it was gradually taking possession of my whole body... The restaurant, my father, the white placard, my sleeves were all smelling of it, smelling so strongly that I began to chew. I moved my jaws and swallowed as though I really had a piece of this marine animal in my mouth.

Anton Chekhov, Oysters, 1884

Fish should smell like the tide. Once they smell like fish, it's too late.

*Oscar Gizelt, food and beverage manager,
Delmonico's restaurant, New York City,
Vogue, April 1964*

COME, follow me by the smell,
Here are delicate onions to sell;
I promise to use you well.
They make the blood warmer,
You'll feed like a farmer;
For this is every cook's opinion,
No savoury dish without an onion;
But, lest your kissing should be spoiled,
Your onions must be thoroughly boiled:
Or else you may spare
Your mistress a share,
The secret will never be known:
She cannot discover
The breath of her lover,
But think it as sweet as her own.

Jonathan Swift, Market Women's Cries, 1720

THE banks of the Sarawak River are everywhere covered with fruit trees, which supply the Dyaks with a great deal of their food. The Mangosteen, Lansat, Rambutan, Jack, Jambou, and Blimbing, are all abundant; but most abundant and most esteemed is the Durian, a fruit about which very little is known in England, but which both by natives and Europeans in the Malay Archipelago is reckoned superior to all others. The old traveller Linschott, writing in 1599, says: "It is of such an excellent taste that it surpasses in flavour all the other fruits of the world, according to those who have tasted it." And Doctor Paludanus adds: "This fruit is of a hot and humid nature. To those not used to it, it seems at first to smell like rotten onions, but immediately when they have tasted it, they prefer it to all other food. The natives give it honourable titles, exalt it, and make verses on it." When brought into a house the smell is often so offensive that some persons can never bear to taste it. This was my own case when I first tried it in Malacca, but in Borneo I found a ripe fruit on the ground, and, eating it out of doors, I at once became a confirmed Durian eater... Its consistency and flavour are indescribable. A rich butter-like custard highly flavoured with almonds gives the best general idea of it, but intermingled with it come wafts of flavour that call to mind cream-cheese, onion-sauce, brown sherry, and other incongruities. Then there is a rich glutinous smoothness in the pulp which nothing else possesses, but which adds to its delicacy. It is neither acid, nor sweet, nor juicy; yet one feels the want of more of these qualities, for it is perfect as it is. It produces no nausea or other bad effect, and the more you eat of it the less you feel inclined to stop. In fact to eat Durians is a new sensation, worth a voyage to the East to experience.

Alfred Russel Wallace, The Malay Archipelago, 1869

THE durian-tree of the East Indies, whose smooth stem often shoots up to a height of eighty or ninety feet without sending out a branch, bears a fruit of the most delicious flavour and the most disgusting stench. The Malays cultivate the tree for the sake of its fruit, and have been known to resort to a peculiar ceremony for the purpose of stimulating its fertility. Near Jugra in Selangor there is a small grove of durian-trees, and on a specially chosen day the villagers used to assemble in it. Thereupon one of the local sorcerers would take a hatchet and deliver several shrewd blows on the trunk of the most barren of the trees, saying, "Will you now bear fruit or not? If you do not, I shall fell you." To this the tree replied through the mouth of another man who had climbed a mangostin-tree hard by (the durian-tree being unclimbable), "Yes, I will now bear fruit; I beg of you not to fell me." So in Japan to make trees bear fruit two men go into an orchard. One of them climbs up a tree and the other stands at the foot with an axe. The man with the axe asks the tree whether it will yield a good crop next year and threatens to cut it down if it does not. To this the man among the branches replies on behalf of the tree that it will bear abundantly.

Sir James George Frazer, The Golden Bough, 1922

THIS manioc meal is the staple food, the bread equivalent, all along the coast...

It is a good food when it is properly prepared; but when a village has soaked its soil-laden manioc tubers in one and the same pool of water for years, the water in that pool becomes a trifle strong, and both it and the manioc get a smell which once smelt is never to be forgotten; it is something like that resulting from bad paste with a dash of vinegar, but fit to pass all these things, and has qualities of its own that have no civilised equivalent.

I believe that this way of preparing the staple article of diet is largely responsible for that dire and frequent disease "cut him belly," and several other quaint disorders, possibly even for the sleep disease. The natives themselves say that a diet too exclusively maniocan produces dimness of vision, ending in blindness if the food is not varied; the poisonous principle cannot be anything like soaked out in the surcharged water, and the meal when it is made up and cooked has just the same sour, acrid taste you would

I thought of her as a large lump of butter, except her smell was not as pleasant. She used a heavy carnation-scented perfume that turned my stomach. I would push her away, saying, "You smell terrible." "Well, you stink of garlic!" my mother would answer. And it was true, since I liked dunking a piece of fresh baguette into a dish of crushed garlic marinating in olive oil and seasoned with salt and pepper....

Aishe, Oman (the valet) and Ahmet would all sit outside in the garden and peel pounds of fresh harvested garlic, which they crushed and minced with salt, then stored in glass jars with a tight lid. The jars sat on the counter amid other jars of black sesame seeds, coriander seeds and cumin seeds. Small, fresh aromatic mint was brought in from the market once every two months. After rinsing the mint several times, Ahmet would spread the leaves on sheets of newspaper to dry in the sun. This would take about a week. He would then pick the dried leave from the stems and rub them between the palms of his hands to crush the mint into powder. He'd open his hands and allow me to smell the strong, sweet aroma of the crushed mint. The powder would be put through a fine sieve before being stored in a glass jar. He used the mint in chicken soup and lentil stew.

Colette Rossant,
Apricots on the Nile, A Memoir with Recipes, 1999

AS for the water, which is said to have effected so many surprising cures, I have drank it once, and the first draught has cured me of all desire to repeat the medicine. – Some people say it smells of rotten eggs, and others compare it to the scourings of a foul gun. – It is generally supposed to be strongly impregnated with sulphur; and Dr Shaw, in his book upon mineral water, says, he has seen flakes of sulphur floating in the well – Pace tanti viri; I, for my part, have never observed any thing like sulphur, either in or about the well, neither do I find that any brimstone has ever been extracted from the water. As for the smell, if I may be allowed to judge from my own organs, it is exactly that of bilge-water; and the saline taste of it seems to declare that it is nothing else than salt water putrified in the bowels of the earth. I was obliged to hold my nose with one hand, while I advanced the glass to my mouth with the other; and after I had made shift to swallow it, my stomach could hardly retain what it had received. – The only effects it produced were sickness, griping, and insurmountable disgust. – I can hardly mention it without puking. – The world is strangely misled by the affectation of singularity. I cannot help suspecting, that this water owes its reputation in a great measure to its being so strikingly offensive. – On the same kind of analogy, a German doctor has introduced hemlock and other poisons, as specifics, into the materia medica. – I am persuaded, that all the cures ascribed to the Harrigate water, would have been as efficaciously, and infinitely more agreeably performed, by the internal and external use of seawater. Sure I am, this last is much less nauseous to the taste and smell, and much more gentle in its operation as a purge, as well as more extensive in its medical qualities.

Tobias Smollett,
The Expedition of Humphry Clinker, 1771

BUT it was the herb garden that Saeeda was most proud of, a small square plot just outside the kitchen door, which she filled with basil and thyme, parsley, mint, rosemary and coriander, everything she loved to touch and smell and taste in her cooking. She spent so much time tending this part of the garden that the heady scents seeped into her clothes and skin, and stayed there so that she had only to lift her hands to her face and the smell of fresh basil mixed with the sharpness of parsley, mint and the exotic aroma of thyme and coriander would fill her nostrils. Villagers said that it was the fragrance emanating from the herb garden that lured the stranger to Saeeda's doorstep one summer afternoon.

Nada Awar Jarrar,
Somewhere, Home, 2003

THE scent of wine, oh how much more agreeable, laughing, praying, celestial and delicious it is than that of oil!

François Rabelais, Gargantua, 1532

CHENIN has a peculiar (and it has to be said, not wholly attractive) bouquet. As well as seeming to smell sweet, no matter what the provenance of the wine, there's a sickly scent to it, like over-ripe soft cheese, coupled with the slightly frowsty smell you get from damp wool drying by a radiator. Damp straw is another association...

*

SAUVIGNON Blanc is a gift in a blind tasting, it has such a powerfully individual character. Nose in glass and instantly you know where you are. It has green associations, like just cut grass and has an unmistakable whiff of gooseberries to it. The gooseberry aroma, if analysed, falls into the same scent spectrum as cats; take a deep sniff of a good sauvignon and you'll see what I mean.

*

GAMAY is ideal for making youthful, vibrant reds as easy to drink as white wine. It's not surprising that fruit – gorgeous, jammy, cherry and raspberry fruit, should lead the scent and flavour medley. If the fruit isn't obvious, you haven't got a very good Gamay in your glass. As well as fruit there is a haunting rubbery sort of aroma to this grape – combined rubber and tar, like gym shoes running on a sun-baked road.

Michael Barry, Jilly Goolden and Peter Bazalgette,
The Big Food and Drink Book, 1993

WEIGHTLESSNESS makes astronauts lose taste and smell in space. In the absence of gravity, molecules cannot be volatile, so few of them get into our noses deeply enough to register as odours. This is a problem for nutritionists designing space food. Much of the taste of food depends on its smell; some chemists have gone so far as to claim that wine is simply a tasteless liquid that is deeply fragrant. Drink wine with a head cold, and you'll taste water, they say. Before something can be tasted, it has to be dissolved in liquid (for example, hard candy has to melt in saliva); and before something can be smelled, it has to be airborne. We taste only four flavours: sweet, sour, salt and bitter. That means that everything else we call "flavour" is really "odour". And many of the foods we think we can smell we can only taste. Sugar isn't volatile, so we don't smell it, even though we taste it intensely. If we have a mouthful of something delicious, which we want to savour and contemplate, we exhale; this drives the air in our mouths across our olfactory receptors, so we can smell it better.

Diane Ackerman, A Natural History of the Senses, 1990

AFTER the "prière du soir", Madame herself came to have another look at me. She desired me to follow her up-stairs. Through a series of the queerest little dormitories – which, I heard afterwards, had once been nuns' cells: for the premises were in part of ancient date – and through the oratory – a long, low, gloomy room, where a crucifix hung, pale, against the wall, and two tapers kept dim vigils – she conducted me to an apartment where three children were asleep in three tiny beds. A heated stove made the air of this room oppressive; and, to mend matters, it was scented with an odour rather strong than delicate: a perfume, indeed, altogether surprising and unexpected under the circumstances, being like the combination of smoke with some spirituous essence – a smell, in short, of whisky.

Charlotte Brontë, Villette, 1853

CHAPTER VIII

"The swooning smells that

lie in the gutters"

The Festering City

FOR the first time he heard his nails click upon the hard paving-stones of London. For the first time the whole battery of a London street on a hot summer's day assaulted his nostrils. He smelt the swooning smells that lie in the gutters; the bitter smells that corrode iron railings; the fuming, heady smells that rise from basements – smells more complex, corrupt, violently contrasted and compounded than any he had smelt in the fields near Reading; smells that lay far beyond the range of the human nose; so that while the chair went on, he stopped, amazed; smelling, savouring, until a jerk at his collar dragged him on.

Virginia Woolf, Flush, 1933

A disgusting, soaked newspaper is wrapped around the feed of fish heads. On the bloody picture the American secretary of state and the Russian foreign minister are shaking hands... The cats are growling and hissing. The old woman throws the paper into the ditch. The severed heads of the oceanic brood, broken eyes, discoloured gills, opalescent scales are thrown among the tail-shipping, meowing pack. Cadavers, a sharp reek of excretion, secretion, copulation, a sweet smell of old rot and pus mounts in the air and mingles with the exhausts of the street and the fresh, stimulating smell of coffee from the espresso bars on the corner of the Piazza della Rotonda.

Wolfgang Koeppen, Death in Rome, 1954

I N Köhln, a town of monks and bones,
  And pavements fang'd with murderous stones
And rags, and hags, and hideous wenches;
I counted two and seventy stenches,
All well defined, and several stinks!
Ye Nymphs that reign o'er sewers and sinks,
The river Rhine, it is well known,
Doth wash your city of Cologne;
But tell me, Nymphs, what power divine
Shall henceforth wash the river Rhine?

Samuel Taylor Coleridge, Cologne, 1828

E VER notice how these European trains always smell of eau de
  cologne and hard boiled eggs?

*Tom in Arise My Love, 1940,
screenplay by Billy Wilder*

M Y chiefest care in choosing my lodgings is always to avoid
  a thick and stinking air; and those beautiful cities, Venice
and Paris, very much lessen the kindness I have for them, the one
by the offensive smell of her marshes, and the other of her dirt.

Michel de Montaigne, Of Smells, 1572-1580

AFTER a few whiffs of another world
he decided to stay with the stench
of the present: dumpster lids everywhere
rising like cakes, garbage scows
moving in long orderly lines
across the harbour... The olfactory – he loves it
even when it wafts, wracking all points
of the compass. It's always invisible
and takes its direction according to the whimsy
of wind, or fans, or the waves
of a hand. Cave dwellers knew it,
and dogs. The bare smell
of dirt on cabbage, the snow-
on-your-arm smell. Even
in the abstract: fear-smell, like spit
on a knife blade. And
what the worms inhale, and then
the smell of dew on barbed-wire, the sweet,
thick smell of sex, slick,
our lungs giddy and pink with it...
It's not the world which is good or bad
and so we run our noses over everything.
even the dumb have this sense.

Thomas Lux,
After a Few Whiffs of Another World, 1980

A warm, odiferous waft of slumdom met them. It was not a smell that could be escaped. There were identifiable odours of cats' urine: decayed rubbish: infectious diseases: unwashed underclothing, intermingled with smells suggesting dry rot: insanitary lavatories, overtaxed sewage pipes and the excrement of a billion bed-bugs.

James Barke, Major Operation, 1936

BEHIND the blistered door, up four flights of dark, brokendown stairs, through zones of smells – stale cooking and wet washing, cats, old clothes, sweat and urine, the odiferous motifs in the symphony of poverty – John and Martine lie sleeping. A shaft of early-morning sun sloping through the skylight slices the room into two twilit halves, and spills over on to the bare floor.

John Sommerfield, May Day, 1936

THE only thing she did not like was the courtyard's dampness. She would want rooms at the rear, on the sunny side. Gervaise took a few more steps into the courtyard, inhaling the characteristic odour of the slums, comprised of dust and rotten garbage. But the sharp odour of the waste water from the dye shop was strong, and Gervaise thought it smelled better here than at the Hotel Boncoeur.

Emile Zola, L'Assommoir, 1877

CONNIE was accustomed to Kensington or the Scotch hills or the Sussex downs: that was her England. With the stoicism of the young she took in the utter, soulless ugliness of the coal-and-iron Midlands at a glance, and left it at what it was: unbelievable and not to be thought about. From the rather dismal rooms at Wragby she heard the rattle-rattle of the screens at the pit, the puff of the winding-engine, the clink-clink of shunting trucks, and the hoarse little whistle of the colliery locomotives. Tevershall pit-bank was burning, had been burning for years, and it would cost thousands to put it out. So it had to burn. And when the wind was that way, which was often, the house was full of the stench of this sulphurous combustion of the earth's excrement. But even on windless days the air always smelt of something under-earth: sulphur, iron, coal, or acid. And even on the Christmas roses the smuts settled persistently, incredible, like black manna from the skies of doom.

D.H. *Lawrence, Lady Chatterley's Lover, 1928*

I have always been particularly sensitive to smells, even squeamish, and when I stepped into that hall I drew my first breath of that medley of mildew, Lysol, ancient grease, rotting woodwork, sweat, rat droppings, coal dust, baby urine and boiled cabbage... the residue of a hundred and fifty years of poverty and hopelessness, damp and eternal in the nostrils.

Trevanian, The Crazyladies of Pearl Street, 2005

THERE was the tough, inert, stuffy air that no wind had dispersed yet... and the exhalations and the age-old smoke and the sweat from the armpits that makes the clothes heavy; the bad breath and the fetid odour of fermenting feet. There was the sharp stench of urine and the burning sensation of soot and the gray steam of potatoes and the heavy, smooth stench of old lard. The sweet, long odour of neglected babies was there too and the smell of fear of school-children, and the sultry haze from the beds of adolscent boys. And many things had accrued from below, evaporated from the abyss of the street; and other smells had filtered down with the rain, which is not clean over the cities. And many things had been accumulated by the tame house-winds that always remain in the same streets, and there were many other things of which one did not know the origin.

Rainer Maria Rilke,
The Notebooks of Malte Laurids Brigge, 1910

CAREFUL observers may foretell the hour
(By sure prognostics) when to dread a shower.
While rain depends, the pensive cat gives o'er
Her frolics, and pursues her tail no more.
Returning home at night, you'll find the sink
Strike your offended sense with double stink.
If you be wise, then go not far to dine,
You spend in coach-hire more than save in wine.
A coming shower your shooting corns presage,
Old aches throb, your hollow tooth will rage.
Sauntering in coffee-house is Dulman seen;
He damns the climate, and complains of spleen.

. . .

Now in contiguous drops the flood comes down,
Threatening with deluge this devoted town.
To shops in crowds the daggled females fly,
Pretend to cheapen Goods, but nothing buy

. . .

Now from all Parts the swelling kennels flow,
And bear their Trophies with them as they go:
Filth of all hues and odours seem to tell
What streets they sailed from, by the sight and smell.
They, as each Torrent drives, with rapid force
From Smithfield, or St. Pulchre's shape their course,
And in huge confluent join at Snow-Hill ridge,
Fall from the conduit prone to Holborn-Bridge.
Sweepings from butchers' stalls, dung, guts, and blood,
Drowned puppies, stinking sprats, all drenched in mud,
Dead cats and turnips-tops come tumbling down the flood.

Jonathan Swift,
A Description of a City Shower, 1710

A heavy moisture hung around, impregnated with a soapy odour, a damp insipid smell, continuous though at moments overpowered by the more potent fumes of the chemicals. Along the washing-places, on either side of the central alley, were rows of women, with bare arms and necks, and skirts tucked up, showing coloured stockings and heavy lace-up shoes. They were beating furiously, laughing, leaning back to call out a word in the midst of the din, or stooping over their tubs, all of them brutal, ungainly, foul of speech, and soaked as though by a shower, with their flesh red and reeking.

...

They went to fetch the bundles in the left hand room where Etienne slept, and returned with enormous armfuls which they piled up on the floor at the back of the shop. The sorting lasted a good half hour... And from all this dirty linen which they were throwing about there issued an offensive odour in the warm atmosphere.

"Oh! La, la. What a stench!" said Clemence, holding her nose.

"Of course there is! If it were clean they wouldn't send it to us," quietly explained Gervaise. "It smells as one would expect it to, that's all! We said fourteen chemises, didn't we, Madame Bijard? Fifteen, sixteen, seventeen – " And she continued counting aloud. Used to this kind of thing she evinced no disgust. She thrust her bare pink arms deep into the piles of laundry: shirts yellow with grime, towels stiff from dirty dish water, socks threadbare and eaten away by sweat. The strong odour which slapped her in the face as she sorted the piles of clothes made her feel drowsy. She seemed to be intoxicating herself with this stench of humanity as she sat on the edge of a stool, bending far over, smiling vaguely, her eyes slightly misty.

...

"It's not for the sake of saying so," he murmured; "but your dirty linen stinks tremendously! Still, I love you all the same, you know."

"Leave off, you're tickling me," cried she, laughing the louder. "What a great silly you are! How can you be so absurd?"

He had caught hold of her and would not let her go. She gradually abandoned herself to him, dizzy from the slight faintness caused by the heap of clothes and not minding Coupeau's foul-smelling breath. The long kiss they exchanged on each other's mouths in the midst of the filth of the laundress's trade was perhaps the first tumble in the slow downfall of their life together.

Emile Zola, L'Assommoir, 1877

BUT the scullery you would not care to see; it is greasy, dirty, and odoriferous, while the stairs are in rags, and the walls so covered with filth that the hand sticks fast wherever it touches them. Also, on each landing there is a medley of boxes, chairs, and dilapidated wardrobes; while the windows have had most of their panes shattered, and everywhere stand washtubs filled with dirt, litter, eggshells, and fish-bladders. The smell is abominable. In short, the house is not a nice one.

As to the disposition of the rooms, I have described it to you already. True, they are convenient enough, yet every one of them has an ATMOSPHERE. I do not mean that they smell badly so much as that each of them seems to contain something which gives forth a rank, sickly-sweet odour. At first the impression is an unpleasant one, but a couple of minutes will suffice to dissipate it, for the reason that EVERYTHING here smells – people's clothes, hands, and everything else – and one grows accustomed to the rankness. Canaries, however, soon die in this house. A naval officer here has just bought his fifth. Birds cannot live long in such an air. Every morning, when fish or beef is being cooked, and washing and scrubbing are in progress, the house is filled with steam. Always, too, the kitchen is full of linen hanging out to dry; and since my room adjoins that apartment, the smell from the clothes causes me not a little annoyance. However, one can grow used to anything.

Fyodor Dostoyevsky, Poor Folk, 1846

JUST beyond the gate of Hyde Park, to the right of the road, stands a cabmen's shelter. Conversation and emotion had made Lord Dreever thirsty. He suggested coffee as a suitable conclusion to the night's revels.

"I often go in here when I'm up in town," he said. "The cabbies don't mind. They're sportsmen."

The shelter was nearly full when they opened the door. It was very warm inside. A cabman gets so much fresh air in the exercise of his professional duties that he is apt to avoid it in private life. The air was heavy with conflicting scents. Fried onions seemed to be having the best of the struggle for the moment, though plug tobacco competed gallantly. A keenly analytical nose might also have detected the presence of steak and coffee.

P.G. Wodehouse, The Intrusion of Jimmy, 1910

THE car slowed down. It had to take its place in the long line of cars that moved at a foot's pace, now stopping dead, now jerking on, down the narrow street, blocked by market carts, that led to the Opera House. Men and women in full evening dress were walking along the pavement. They looked uncomfortable and self-conscious… She leant back in her corner. Covent Garden porters, dingy little clerks in their ordinary working clothes, coarse-looking women in aprons stared in at her. The air smelt strongly of oranges and bananas. But the car was coming to a standstill. It drew up under the archway; she pushed through the glass doors and went in. She felt at once a sense of relief… The ladies and gentlemen who were mounting the stairs were dressed exactly as she was. The smell of oranges and bananas had been replaced by another smell – a subtle mixture of clothes and gloves and flowers that affected her pleasantly.

Virginia Woolf, The Years, 1937

LIKE a wind that swells in a steady roar, I heard with joy a car beneath the window. I sniffed its smell of petrol. The latter may seem regrettable to the oversensitive (who are always materialists and for whom it spoils the country)... But to me (just as an aroma, unpleasing perhaps in itself, of naphthalene and vetiver would have thrilled me by bringing back to me the blue purity of the sea on the day of my arrival at Balbec), this smell of petrol which, together with the smoke from the exhaust of the car, had so often melted into the pale azure on those scorching days when I used to drive from Saint-Jean-de-la-Haise to Gourville, since it had accompanied me on my excursions during those summer afternoons when I left Albertine painting, called into blossom now on either side of me, for all that I was lying in my darkened bedroom, corn-flowers, poppies and red clover, intoxicated me like a country scent.

Marcel Proust, The Captive, 1923

LA has its own smell. One I've always liked very much – flowers, heat and freshness, with a vinaigrette dressing of gasoline over the top.

Jonathan Carroll, White Apples Journal, 2002

YES, New York looked good ... good and exciting, with all the taxi-cabs rattling in at the dark tunnel beside her, with all the people hurrying in and hurrying out, with all this medley of street-cars and sky-signs and crushed snow and drays and horses and policemen, and that vast hotel across the street, towering to heaven like a cliff. It even smelt good. She remembered an old picture in Punch, of two country visitors standing on the step of their railway carriage at a London terminus, one saying ecstatically to other: "Don't speak! Just sniff! Doesn't it smell of the Season!" She knew exactly how they had felt, and she approved of their attitude. That was the right way to behave on being introduced to a great metropolis. She stood and sniffed reverently. But for the presence of the hurrying crowds, she could almost have imitated the example of that king who kissed the soil of his country on landing from his ship.

P.G. Wodehouse, The Little Warrior, 1920

SO she came out of the dressing-room at Delmonico's and stood for a second in the doorway looking over the shoulders of a black dress in front of her at the groups of Yale men who flitted like dignified black moths around the head of the stairs. From the room she had left drifted out the heavy fragrance left by the passage to and fro of many scented young beauties – rich perfumes and the fragile memory-laden dust of fragrant powders. This odor drifting out acquired the tang of cigarette smoke in the hall, and then settled sensuously down the stairs and permeated the ballroom where the Gamma Psi dance was to be held. It was an odor she knew well, exciting, stimulating, restlessly sweet – the odor of a fashionable dance.

F. Scott Fitzgerald, Tales of the Jazz Age, 1922

MUFFAT was beginning to perspire; he had taken his hat off. What inconvenienced him most was the stuffy, dense, overheated air of the place with its strong, haunting smell, a smell peculiar to this part of a theatre, and, as such, compact of the reek of gas, of the glue used in the manufacture of the scenery, of dirty dark nooks and corners and of questionably clean chorus girls. In the passage the air was still more suffocating, and one seemed to breathe a poisoned atmosphere, which was occasionally relieved by the acid scents of toilet waters and the perfumes of various soaps emanating from the dressing rooms. The count lifted his eyes as he passed and glanced up the staircase, for he was well-nigh startled by the keen flood of light and warmth which flowed down upon his back and shoulders. High up above him there was a clicking of ewers and basins, a sound of laughter and of people calling to one another, a banging of doors, which in their continual opening and shutting allowed an odour of womankind to escape – a musky scent of oils and essences mingling with the natural pungency exhaled from human tresses. He did not stop. Nay, he hastened his walk: he almost ran, his skin tingling with the breath of that fiery approach to a world he knew nothing of.

Emile Zola, Nana, 1880

THESE sequestered nooks are the public offices of the legal profession, where writs are issued, judgments signed, declarations filed, and numerous other ingenious machines put in motion for the torture and torment of His Majesty's liege subjects, and the comfort and emolument of the practitioners of the law. They are, for the most part, low-roofed, mouldy rooms, where innumerable rolls of parchment, which have been perspiring in secret for the last century, send forth an agreeable odour, which is mingled by day with the scent of the dry-rot, and by night with the various exhalations which arise from damp cloaks, festering umbrellas, and the coarsest tallow candles.

Charles Dickens, The Pickwick Papers, 1837

CHAPTER IX

"Watermelons bedded in sweet hay"

Dung and Roses

O, how much more doth beauty beauteous seem
By that sweet ornament which truth doth give!
The rose looks fair, but fairer we it deem
For that sweet odor which doth in it live.
The canker-blooms have full as deep a dye
As the perfumed tincture of the roses,
Hang on such thorns and play as wantonly
When summer's breath their masked buds discloses;
But for their virtue only is their show,
They live unwoo'd, and unrespected fade,
Die to themselves. Sweet roses do not so,
Of their sweet deaths are sweetest odors made:
And so of you, beauteous and lovely youth,
When that shall vade, by verse distills your truth.

William Shakespeare, Sonnet 54, c1600

PERFUMERS and flavourists are constantly humbled by the greatest perfumer of them all, Nature. A walk through a rose garden in June will reveal every varietal to have a unique smell, ranging from that peculiarly lemony style which one never encounters in perfume, to the heavy oriental via all shades of peppery tea. A ripe mango, with its combination of incense-like austerity and sulphurous decadence, is a perfumery idea of pure genius. The exhaust blast from the coffee-roasting shop down the street is as rich and beautiful as anything bottled by man. That is probably why most perfumers see themselves as craftsmen, not artists.

Luca Turin, The Secret of Scent,
Adventures in Perfume and the Science of Smell, 2006

THE scent of an apple as a young girl bites it, the fragrance that comes from Corycian saffron, the smell of a silvery vineyard flowering with the first clusters of grass that a sheep has freshly cropped, the odour of myrtle, of an Arabian harvester, of rubbed amber, of fire pallid with eastern incense, of turf lightly sprinkled with summer rain.

Martial, Epigrams, c90

I cannot see what flowers are at my feet,
Nor what soft incense hangs upon the boughs,
But, in embalmed darkness, guess each sweet
Wherewith the seasonable month endows
The grass, the thicket, and the fruit-tree wild;
White hawthorn, and the pastoral eglantine;
Fast fading violets cover'd up in leaves;
And mid-May's eldest child,
The coming musk-rose, full of dewy wine,
The murmurous haunt of flies on summer eves.
I cannot see what flowers are at my feet,
Nor what soft incense hangs upon the boughs,
But, in embalmèd darkness, guess each sweet
Wherewith the seasonable month endows
The grass, the thicket, and the fruit-tree wild;
White hawthorn, and the pastoral eglantine;
Fast-fading violets cover'd up in leaves;
And mid-May's eldest child,
The coming musk-rose, full of dewy wine,
The murmurous haunt of flies on summer eves.

John Keats, Ode to a Nightingale, 1819

FOR one moment, being afraid of fainting away under
the influence of those feminine odours which he now re-
encountered, intensified by the heat under the low-pitched ceiling,
he sat down on the edge of a softly padded divan between the two
windows. But he got up again almost directly and, returning to
the dressing table, seemed to gaze with vacant eyes into space, for
he was thinking of a bouquet of tuberoses which had once faded
in his bedroom and had nearly killed him in their death. When
tuberoses are turning brown they have a human smell.

Emile Zola, Nana, 1889

"WHERE have you been?" he would call to her, taking hold of her arms, and feeling her skirts, her bodice, and her cheeks. "You smell of all sorts of nice things. Ah! you have been walking on the grass?" At this she would laugh and show him her shoes wet with dew.

"You have been in the garden! you have been in the garden!" he then exclaimed delightedly. "I knew it. When you came in you seemed like a large flower. You have brought the whole garden in your skirt."

He would keep her by him, inhaling her like a nosegay. Sometimes she came back with briars, leaves, or bits of wood entangled in her clothes. These he would remove and hide under his pillow like relics. One day she brought him a bunch of roses. At the sight of them he was so affected that he wept. He kissed them and went to sleep with them in his arms. But when they faded, he felt so keenly grieved that he forbade Albine to gather any more. He preferred her, said he, for she was as fresh and as balmy; and she never faded, her hands, her hair, her cheeks were always fragrant. At last he himself would send her into the garden, telling her not to come back before an hour.

"In that way," he said, "I shall get sunlight, fresh air, and roses till tomorrow."

Emile Zola, The Sin of the Abbé Mouret, 1875

NOW whenas sacred light began to dawn
In Eden on the humid flow'rs, that breathedd
Their morning incense, when all things that breathe,
From th'earths great altar send up silent praise
To the Creator, and his nostrils fill
With grateful smell, forth came the human pair
And joined their vocal worship to the choir
Of creatures wanting voice, that done, partake
The season, prime for sweetest scents and airs.

John Milton, Paradise Lost, 1667

AND because the breath of flowers is far sweeter in the air (where it comes and goes like the warbling of music) than in the hand, therefore nothing is more fit for that delight, than to know what be the flowers and plants that do best perfume the air. Roses, damask and red, are fast flowers of their smells; so that you may walk by a whole row of them, and find nothing of their sweetness; yea though it be in a morning's dew. Bays likewise yield no smell as they grow. Rosemary little; nor sweet marjoram. That which above all others yields the sweetest smell in the air is the violet, specially the white double violet, which comes twice a year; about the middle of April, and about Bartholomew-tide. Next to that is the musk-rose. Then the strawberry-leaves dying, which yield a most excellent cordial smell. Then the flower of the vines; it is a little dust, like the dust of a bent, which grows upon the cluster in the first coming forth. Then sweet-briar. Then wall-flowers, which are very delightful to be set under a parlor or lower chamber window. Then pinks and gilliflowers, especially the matted pink and clove gilliflower. Then the flowers of the lime-tree. Then the honeysuckles, so they be somewhat afar off. Of bean-flowers I speak not, because they are field flowers. But those which perfume the air most delightfully, not passed by as the rest, but being trodden upon and crushed, are three; that is, burnet, wild-thyme, and watermints. Therefore you are to set whole alleys of them, to have the pleasure when you walk or tread.

Francis Bacon, Of Gardens, 1625

WE never named musk in her presence, her antipathy to it was so well understood through the household: her opinion on the subject was believed to be, that no scent derived from an animal could ever be of a sufficiently pure nature to give pleasure to any person of good family, where, of course, the delicate perception of the senses had been cultivated for generations. She would instance the way in which sportsmen preserve the breed of dogs who have shown keen scent; and how such gifts descend for generations amongst animals, who cannot be supposed to have anything of ancestral pride, or hereditary fancies about them. Musk, then, was never mentioned at Hanbury Court...

For lasting vegetable odours she preferred lavender and sweet-woodroof to any extract whatever. Lavender reminded her of old customs, she said, and of homely cottage-gardens, and many a cottager made his offering to her of a bundle of lavender. Sweet woodroof, again, grew in wild, woodland places where the soil was fine and the air delicate: the poor children used to go and gather it for her up in the woods on the higher lands; and for this service she always rewarded them with bright new pennies, of which my lord, her son, used to send her down a bagful fresh from the Mint in London every February. Attar of roses, again, she disliked. She said it reminded her of the city and of merchants' wives, over-rich, over-heavy in its perfume. And lilies-of-the-valley somehow fell under the same condemnation. They were most graceful and elegant to look at (my lady was quite candid about this), flower, leaf, colour – everything was refined about them but the smell. That was too strong. But the great hereditary faculty on which my lady piqued herself, and with reason, for I never met with any person who possessed it, was the power she had of perceiving the delicious odour arising from a bed of strawberries in the late autumn, when the leaves were all fading and dying. "Bacon's Essays" was one of the few books that lay about in my lady's room; and if you took it up and opened it carelessly, it was sure to fall apart at his "Essay on Gardens." "Listen," her ladyship would say, "to what that great philosopher and statesman says. 'Next to that,' – he is speaking of violets, my dear – 'is the musk-rose,' – of which you remember the great bush, at the corner of the south wall just by the Blue Drawing-room windows; that is the old musk-rose, Shakespeare's musk-rose, which is dying out through the kingdom now. But to return to my Lord Bacon: 'Then the strawberry leaves, dying with a most excellent cordial smell.' Now the Hanburys can always smell this excellent cordial odour, and very delicious and refreshing it is."

Elizabeth Gaskell, My Lady Ludlow, 1859

YOU never sent (in a dream)
the very form, the very scent,
not heavy, not sensuous,
but perilous – perilous –
of orchids, piled in a great sheath,
and folded underneath on a bright scroll
some word:

Flower sent to flower;
for white hands, the lesser white,
less lovely of flower leaf

H.D. (Hilda Doolittle), At Baia, 1921

YOU like orchids? ... Nasty things. Their flesh is too much like
the flesh of men, their perfume has the rotten sweetness of
corruption.

William Faulkner, Leigh Brackett, Jules Furthmann
and Howard Hawks, The Big Sleep, 1946

THROUGH the open door, stealthily, came the scent of madonna lilies, almost as if it were prowling abroad. Suddenly he got up and went out of doors.

The beauty of the night made him want to shout. A half–moon, dusky gold, was sinking behind the black sycamore at the end of the garden, making the sky dull purple with its glow. Nearer, a dim white fence of lilies went across the garden, and the air all round seemed to stir with scent, as if it were alive. He went across the bed of pinks, whose keen perfume came sharply across the rocking, heavy scent of the lilies, and stood alongside the white barrier of flowers. They flagged all loose, as if they were panting. The scent made him drunk. He went down to the field to watch the moon sink under.

A corncrake in the hay-close called insistently. The moon slid quite quickly downwards, growing more flushed. Behind him the great flowers leaned as if they were calling. And then, like a shock, he caught another perfume, something raw and coarse. Hunting round, he found the purple iris, touched their fleshy throats and their dark, grasping hands. At any rate, he had found something. They stood stiff in the darkness. Their scent was brutal. The moon was melting down upon the crest of the hill. It was gone; all was dark. The corncrake called still.

Breaking off a pink, he suddenly went indoors.

D.H. Lawrence, Sons and Lovers, 1913

C'EST le couchant. O prodige, une singulière rougeur, autour de laquelle se répand une odeur énivrante de chevelures secouées, tombe en cascade du ciel obscure! Est-ce une avalanche de roses mauvaises ayant le péché pour parfum?

[The sun is setting. Oh, what a miracle, a spectacular red, around which a dizzying odour of loosened hair is spreading, cascading from the darkening sky! Is it an avalanche of evil roses steeped in the odour of sin?]

Stéphane Mallarmé, Proses de Jeunesse II, 1854

THE fairest things have fleetest end,
    Their scent survives their close:
But the rose's scent is bitterness
To him that loved the rose.

Francis Thompson, Daisy, 1893

FEW people have been as obsessed with roses as the ancient Romans. Roses were strewn at public ceremonies and banquets; rose water bubbled throught the emperor's fountains and the public baths surged with it; in the public ampitheatres, crowds sat under sun awnings steeped in rose perfume; rose petals were used as pillow stuffings; people wore garlands of roses in their hair; they ate rose pudding; their medicines, love potions, and aphrodisiacs all contained roses. No bacchanalia, the Romans' official orgy, was complete without an excess of roses. They created a holiday, Rosalia, to formally consummate their passion for the flower. At one banquet, Nero had silver pipes installed under each plate, so that guests could be spritzed with scent between courses. They could admire a ceiling painted to resemble the celestial heavens, which would open up and shower them in a continuous rain of perfume and flowers. At another, he spent the equivalent of $160,000 just on roses – and one of his guests smothered to death under a shower of rose petals.

Diane Ackerman, , A Natural History of the Senses, 1990

BUT it chanced the other day that I scented a white water-lily... It is the emblem of purity... What confirmation of our hopes is in the fragrance of this flower! I shall not so soon despair of the world for it, notwithstanding slavery, and the cowardice and want of principle of Northern men. It suggests what kinds of laws have prevailed longest and widest, and still prevail, and that the time may come when man's deeds will smell as sweet. Such is the odor which the plant emits... It reminds me that Nature has been partner to no Missouri compromise. I scent no compromise in the fragrance of the water-lily.

Henry David Thoreau, Slavery in Massachusetts, 1854

OF the great fragrance that entered my heart
when I kissed the precious and sweet-smelling Flower,
I am unable to speak or tell;
but I will tell how the sea became tempestuous
because of Bad Mouth, that Norman thief,
who saw the event and awakened Jealousy
and Chastity, for they were sleeping;
for this reason I was again cast out of the garden.

Dante Alghieri, Fiore, c1300

WE entered the farmhouse. The smoky kitchen was high and spacious. The copper utensils and the crockery shone in the reflection of the hearth. A cat lay asleep on a chair, a dog under the table. One perceived an odour of milk, apples, smoke, that indescribable smell peculiar to old farmhouses; the odour of the earth, of the walls, of furniture, the odour of spilled stale soup, of former wash-days and of former inhabitants, the smell of animals and of human beings combined, of things and of persons, the odour of time, and of things that have passed away.

Guy de Maupassant, The Farmer's Wife, 1886

A dunghill at a distance sometimes smells like musk, & a dead dog like elder-flowers.

Samuel Taylor Coleridge, Notebooks, 1797

"**O** base transmutation!" exclaimed his antagonist; "thou hast already got the true rustic slouch – thy shoulders stoop, as if thine hands were at the stilts of the plough; and thou hast a kind of earthy smell about thee, instead of being perfumed with essence, as a gallant and courtier should. On my soul, thou hast stolen out to roll thyself on a hay mow! Thy only excuse will be to swear by thy hilts that the farmer had a fair daughter."

Sir Walter Scott, Kenilworth, 1821

FROM above us, from every side, came the happy songs of little birds calling to one another among the dripping brushwood, while clear from the inmost depths of the wood sounded the voice of the cuckoo. So delicious was the wondrous scent of the wood, the scent which follows a thunderstorm in spring, the scent of birch-trees, violets, mushrooms, and thyme, that I could no longer remain in the britchka. Jumping out, I ran to some bushes, and, regardless of the showers of drops discharged upon me, tore off a few sprigs of thyme, and buried my face in them to smell their glorious scent.

Then, despite the mud which had got into my boots, as also the fact that my stockings were soaked, I went skipping through the puddles to the window of the carriage.

"Lubotshka! Katenka!" I shouted as I handed them some of the thyme, "Just look how delicious this is!"

The girls smelt it and cried, "A-ah!" but Mimi shrieked to me to go away, for fear I should be run over by the wheels.

"Oh, but smell how delicious it is!" I persisted.

Leo Tolstoy, Boyhood, 1854

COLLINS Street was now as empty as a bush road. The young people went into Bourke Street, where, for want of something better to do, they entered the Eastern Market and strolled about inside. The noise that rose from the livestock, on ground floor and upper storey, was ear-splitting: pigs grunted; cocks crowed, turkeys gobbled, parrots shrieked; while rough human voices echoed and re-echoed under the lofty roof. There was a smell, too, an extraordinary smell, composed of all the individual smells of all these living things: of fruit and vegetables, fresh and decayed; of flowers, and butter, and grain; of meat, and fish, and strong cheeses; of sawdust sprinkled with water, and freshly wet pavements – one great complicated smell, the piquancy of which made Laura sniff like a spaniel. But after a very few minutes Tilly, whose temper was still short, called it a "vile stink" and clapped her handkerchief to her nose, and so they hurried out, past many enticing little side booths hidden in dark corners on the ground floor, such as a woman without legs, a double-headed calf, and the like.

Henry Handel Richardson, The Getting of Wisdom, 1910

THERE were rooms of that country order which... enchant us with the countless odours emanating from the virtues, wisdom, habits, a whole secret system of life, invisible, superabundant and profoundly moral, which their atmosphere holds in solution; smells natural enough indeed, and weather-tinted like those of the neighbouring countryside, but already humanised, domesticated, snug, an exquisite, limpid jelly skilfully blended from all the fruits of the year which have left the orchard for the store-room, smells changing with the season, but plenishing and homely, offsetting the sharpness of hoarfrost with the sweetness of warm bread, smells lazy and punctual as a village clock, roving and settled, heedless and provident, linen smells, morning smells, pious smells, rejoicing in a peace which brings only additional anxiety, and in a prosaicness which serves as a deep reservoir of poetry to the stranger who passes through their midst without having lived among them.

Marcel Proust, Swann's Way, 1913

HE knew the inchoate sharp excitement of hot dandelions in young spring grass at noon; the smell of cellars, cobwebs, and built-on secret earth; in July, of watermelons bedded in sweet hay, inside a farmer's covered wagon; of cantaloupe and crated peaches; and the scent of orange rind bittersweet, before a fire of coals. He knew the good male smell of his father's sitting room, of the smooth worn leather sofa, with the gaping horsehair rent, of the blistered varnished wood upon the hearth; of the heated calfskin bindings; of the flat moist plug of Apple tobacco, stuck with a red flag; of woodsmoke and burnt leaves in October; of the brown tired autumn earth; of honeysuckle at night; of warm nasturtiums; of a clean ruddy farmer who comes weekly with printed butter, eggs, and milk... the smell of stored apples in the cellar, and of orchard-apple smells, of pressed cider pulp; of pears ripening on a sunny shelf, and of ripe cherries stewing with sugar on hot stoves before preserving; the smell of whittled wood, of all young lumber, of sawdust and shavings; of peaches stuck with cloves and pickled in brandy; of pine sap, and green pine needles; of a horse's pared hoof; of chestnuts roasting... of foul weeds rotting in green marsh scum; and the exquisite smell of the South, clean but funky, like a big woman; of soaking trees and the earth after heavy rain

Yes, and the smell of hot daisyfields in the morning; of melted pudding iron in a foundry; the winter smell of horsewarm stables and smoking dung; of old oak and walnut; and the butcher's smell of meat, of strong slaughtered lamb... and the lush undergrowth smell of Southern hills; of a slimy oyster can, of chilled gutted fish; of a hot kitchen Negress; of kerosene and moist loin smell of women, and their strong pitted armstench; and the smell of the wind and the rain; and of the acrid thunder; of cold starlight, and the brittle-bladed frozen grass; of fog and the misted winter sun; of seed time, bloom, and mellow dropping harvest.

Thomas Wolfe, O Lost: A Story of the Buried Life, 1929

WE have lunch under the tigli almost every day. Their blossoms are like pearly earrings dangling from the leaves, and when they open – all it seems on the same day – fragrance envelops the whole hillside. At the height of bloom, we sit on the upstairs patio, just adjacent to the trees, trying to identify the fragrance. I think it smells like the perfume counter in the dime store; Ed thinks it smells like the oil his uncle Syl used to slick back his hair. Either way, it attracts every bee in town.

Frances Mayes, Under the Tuscan Sun:
At Home in Italy, 1997

JON got out, then, and she unlatched the footpath gate. They stood a minute within, listening for sounds of anyone to interrupt their trespass. The fine September afternoon was dying fast. The last "sitting" had been long, and it was late; and in the coppice of larch and birch the dusk was deepening. Fleur slid her hand within his arm.

"Listen! Still, isn't it? I feel as if we were back seven years, Jon. Do you wish we were? Babes in the wood once more?"

Gruffly he answered: "No good looking back – things happen as they must."

"The birds are going to bed. Used there to be owls?"

"Yes; we shall hear one soon, I expect."

"How good it smells!"

"Trees and the cow-houses!"

"Vanilla and hay, as the poets have it. Are they close?"

"Yes."

"Don't let's go further, then."

"Here's the old log," said Jon. "We might sit down, and listen for an owl."

On the old log seat they sat down, side by side.

"No dew," said Fleur. "The weather will break soon, I expect. I love the scent of drought."

"I love the smell of rain."

"You and I never love the same thing, Jon. And yet – we've loved each other." Against her arm it was as if he shivered.

John Galsworthy, Swan Song, 1928

A ND surely of all smells in the world, the smell of many trees is the sweetest and most fortifying. The sea has a rude, pistolling sort of odour, that takes you in the nostrils like snuff, and carries with it a fine sentiment of open water and tall ships; but the smell of a forest, which comes nearest to this in tonic quality, surpasses it by many degrees in the quality of softness. Again, the smell of the sea has little variety, but the smell of a forest is infinitely changeful; it varies with the hour of the day, not in strength merely, but in character; and the different sorts of trees, as you go from one zone of the wood to another, seem to live among different kinds of atmosphere. Usually the resin of the fir predominates. But some woods are more coquettish in their habits; and the breath of the forest of Mormal, as it came aboard upon us that showery afternoon, was perfumed with nothing less delicate than sweetbrier.

Robert Louis Stevenson, An Inland Voyage, 1878

O NE bright December mid-day lately I spent down on the New Jersey sea-shore, reaching it by a little more than an hour's railroad trip over the old Camden and Atlantic. I had started betimes, fortified by nice strong coffee and a good breakfast (cook'd by the hands I love, my dear sister Lou's – how much better it makes the victuals taste, and then assimilate, strengthen you, perhaps make the whole day comfortable afterwards.) Five or six miles at the last, our track enter'd a broad region of salt grass meadows, intersected by lagoons, and cut up everywhere by watery runs. The sedgy perfume, delightful to my nostrils, reminded me of "the mash" and south bay of my native island. I could have journey'd contentedly till night through these flat and odorous sea-prairies.

Walt Whitman, A Winter Day
on the Sea-Beach, Specimen Days, 1882

THE rain of winter is dense, hard, compressed. In the spring it has new vitality. It is light, mobile, and laden with a thousand palpitating odors from earth, grass and sprouting leaves. The air of midsummer is dense, saturated, or dry and burning, as if it came from a furnace. When a cool breeze brushes the sultry stillness, it brings fewer odors than in May, and frequently the odor of a coming tempest. The avalanche of coolness which sweeps through the low-hanging air bears little resemblance to the stinging coolness of winter.

The rain of winter is raw, without odor and dismal. The rain of spring is brisk, fragrant, charged with life-giving warmth. I welcome it delightedly as it visits the earth, enriches the streams, waters the hills abundantly, makes the furrows soft with showers for the seed, elicits a perfume which I cannot breathe deep enough. Spring rain is beautiful, impartial, lovable. With pearly drops it washes every leaf on tree and bush, ministers equally to salutary herbs and noxious growths, searches out every living thing that needs its beneficence.

The senses assist and reinforce each other to such an extent that I am not sure whether touch or smell tells me the most about the world. Everywhere the river or touch is joined by the brooks of odor-perception. Each season has its distinctive odors. The spring is earthy and full of sap. July is rich with the odor of ripening grain and hay. As the season advances, a crisp, dry, mature odor predominates, and golden-rod, tansy, and everlastings mark the onward march of the year. In autumn, soft, alluring scents fill the air, floating from thicket, grass, flower, and tree, and they tell me of time and change, of death and life's renewal, desire and its fulfilment.

Helen Keller, Sense and Sensibility, 1907

IN the spring, at the end of the day, you should smell like dirt.

Attributed to Margaret Atwood, c1980

A delicate odour is borne on the wings of the morning breeze,
The odour of leaves, and of grass, and of newly up-turned earth, The birds are singing for joy of the Spring's glad birth,
  Hopping from branch to branch on the rocking trees.

Oscar Wilde, Magdalen Walks, 1881

SOFT as the bed in the earth
  Where a stone has lain –
So soft, so smooth and so cool,
Spring closes me in
With her arms and her hands.

Rich as the smell
Of new earth on a stone,
That has lain, breathing
The damp through its pores –
Spring closes me in
With her blossomy hair;
Brings dark to my eyes.

William Carlos Williams, The Shadow, 1917

BOYS are wild animals, rich in the treasures of sense, but the New England boy had a wider range of emotions than boys of more equable climates. He felt his nature crudely, as it was meant. To the boy Henry Adams, summer was drunken. Among senses, smell was the strongest: – smell of hot pine-woods and sweet-fern in the scorching summer noon; of new-mown hay; of ploughed earth; of box hedges; of peaches, lilacs, syringes; of stables, barns, cow-yards; of salt water and low tide on the marshes; nothing came amiss.

Henry Adams, The Education of Henry Adams, 1907

L O, 'tis autumn;
Lo, where the trees, deeper green, yellower and redder,
Cool and sweeten Ohio's villages, with leaves fluttering in the
moderate wind,
Where apples ripe in the orchards hang, and grapes on the trellis'd
vines;
(Smell you the smell of the grapes on the vines?
Smell you the buckwheat, where the bees were lately buzzing?)

Above all, lo, the sky so calm, so transparent after the rain, and
with wondrous clouds,
Below, too, all calm, all vital and beautiful, and the farm prospers
well.

Walt Whitman, Come up from the Fields, Father,
in Leaves of Grass, 1855

L OW – low
Over a perishing after-glow,
A thin, red shred of moon
Trailed. In the windless air
The poplars all ranked lean and chill.
The smell of winter loitered there,
And the Year's heart felt still.

William Ernest Henley, Low – low, c1872

T HE whole great room was filled with the fragrance of slightly
singed evergreen twigs and glowing with light from countless
tiny flames. The sky-blue hangings with the white figures on them
added to the brilliance. There stood the mighty tree, between
the dark red window-curtains, towering nearly to the ceiling,
decorated with silver tinsel and large white lilies, with a shining
angel at the top and the manger at the foot... They had all eaten
the midday meal earlier than usual today, and been hungry for
the tea and biscuits. But they had scarcely finished when great
crystal bowls were handed round full of a yellow, grainy substance
which turned out to be almond cream... The lights of the great
tree were now burnt down and extinguished, the manger was in

darkness. But a few candles still burned on the small trees, and now and then a twig came within reach of the flame and crackled up, increasing the pungent smell in the room. Every breath of air that stirred the trees stirred the pieces of tinsel too, and made them give out a delicate metallic whisper... Hanno abandoned himself to the enjoyment of the Christmas sounds and smells.

Thomas Mann, Buddenbrooks, 1902

FORGET scented candles and freshly brewed coffee. Every home should smell of baking Christmas cake. That, and warm freshly ironed tea towels hanging on the rail in front of the Aga. It was a pity we had Auntie Fanny living with us. Her incontinence could take the edge off the smell of a chicken curry, let alone a baking cake. No matter how many mince pies were being made, or pine logs burning in the grate, or how many orange-and-clove pomanders my mother had made, there was always the faintest whiff of Aunt Fanny.

Warm sweet fruit, a cake in the oven, woodsmoke, warm ironing, hot retriever curled up by the Aga, mince pies, Mum's 4711. Every child's Christmas memories should smell like that. Mine did. It is a pity that there was always a passing breeze of ammonia.

Nigel Slater, Toast, 2003

DARK and dull night, flie hence away,
And give the honor to this day
That sees December turn'd to May.

. . .

Why does the chilling winter's morne
Smile like a field beset with corn?
Or smell like to a meade new-shorne,
Thus on the sudden? – Come and see
The cause why things thus fragrant be.

Robert Herrick, A Christmas Carol
Sung to the King in the Presence at White-Hall, 1647

CHAPTER X

"I know the grass beyond the door,
The sweet keen smell"

Remembered Fragrances

I have been here before,
But when or how I can not tell;
I know the grass beyond the door,
The sweet keen smell,
The sighing sound, the lights around the shore.

Dante Gabriel Rossetti,
Sudden Light, 1881

IT occasionally happens that, for no particular reason, long-forgotten scenes suddenly start up in the memory. This may in many cases be due to the action of some hardly perceptible odour, which accompanied those scenes and now recurs exactly the same as before. For it is well known that the sense of smell is specially effective in awakening memories, and that in general it does not require much to rouse a train of ideas. And I may say, in passing, that the sense of sight is connected with the understanding, the sense of hearing with the reason, and, as we see in the present case, the sense of smell with the memory. Touch and Taste are more material and dependent upon contact. They have no ideal side.

Arthur Schopenhauer,
Studies in Pessimism, 1851

OLD Man, or Lads-Love, – in the name there's nothing
 To one that knows not Lads-Love, or Old Man,
The hoar green feathery herb, almost a tree,
Growing with rosemary and lavender.
Even to one that knows it well, the names
Half decorate, half perplex, the thing it is:
At least, what that is clings not to the names
In spite of time. And yet I like the names.

The herb itself I like not, but for certain
I love it, as someday the child will love it
Who plucks a feather from the door-side bush
Whenever she goes in or out of the house.
Often she waits there, snipping the tips and shrivelling
The shreds at last on to the path, perhaps
Thinking, perhaps of nothing, till she sniffs
Her fingers and runs off. The bush is still
But half as tall as she, though it is not old;
So well she clips it. Not a word she says;
And I can only wonder how much hereafter
She will remember, with that bitter scent,
Of garden rows, and ancient damson trees
Topping a hedge, a bent path to a door
A low thick bush beside the door, and me
Forbidding her to pick.
                                        As for myself,
Where first I met the bitter scent is lost.
I, too, often shrivel the grey shreds,
Sniff them and think and sniff again and try
Once more to think what it is I am remembering,
Always in vain. I cannot like the scent,
Yet I would rather give up others more sweet,
With no meaning, than this bitter one.
I have mislaid the key. I sniff the spray
And think of nothing; I see and I hear nothing;
Yet seem, too, to be listening, lying in wait
For what I should, yet never can, remember:

No garden appears, no path, no hoar-green bush
Of Lad's-love, or Old Man, no child beside,
Neither father nor mother, nor any playmate;
Only an avenue, dark, nameless, without end.

Edward Thomas, Old Man, 1914

THE Méséglise and Guermantes ways left me exposed, in later life, to much disillusionment and even to many mistakes. For often I have wished to see a person again without realising that it was simply because that person recalled to be a hedge of hawthorns in blossom... But by the same token, and by their persistence in those of my present-day impressions to which they can still be linked, they give those impressions a foundation, a depth, a dimension lacking from the rest. They invest them, too, with a charm, a significance which is for me alone. When, on a summer evening, the melodious sky growls like a tawny lion, and everyone is complaining of the strorm, it is the memory of the Méséglise way that makes me stand alone in ecstasy, inhaling, through the noise of the falling rain, the lingering scent of invisible lilacs.

...

It was in vain that I lingered beside the hawthorns – breathing in their invisible and unchanging odour, trying to fix it in my mind (which did not know what to do with it), losing it, recapturing it, absorbing myself in the rhythm which disposed the flowers here and there with a youthful lightheartedness and at intervals as unexpected as certain intervals in music – they went on offering me the same charm in inexhaustible profusion, but without letting me delve any more deeply, like those melodies which one can play a hundred times in succession without coming any nearer their secret.

Marcel Proust, Swann's Way, 1913

SHE had entirely lost her sense of smell and was almost continuously pursued by one or two subjective olfactory sensations. She found these most distressing...when I asked her what the smell was by which she was most constantly troubled she answered: "A smell of burnt pudding." Thus I only needed to assume that a smell of burnt pudding had actually occurred in the experience which had operated as a trauma... I asked her if she could remember the occasion on which she first had the smell of burnt pudding. "Oh yes, I know exactly. It was about two months ago, two days before my birthday. I was with the children in the schoolroom and was playing at cooking with them" (they were two little girls). "A letter was brought in that had just been left by the postman. I saw from the postmark and the handwriting that it was from my mother in Glasgow and wanted to open it and read it; but the children rushed at me, tore the letter out of my hands and cried: "No, you shan't read it now! It must be for your birthday; we'll keep it for you!" While the children were having this game with me there was suddenly a strong smell. They had forgotten the pudding they were cooking and it was getting burnt. Ever since then I have been pursued by the smell. It is there all the time and becomes stronger when I am agitated."

"Do you see this scene clearly before your eyes?" – "As large as life, just as I experienced it." – "What could there be about it that was so agitating?" – "I was moved because the children were so affectionate to me... I was intending to go back to my mother's, and the thought of leaving the dear children made me feel sad."... This seemed to complete the analysis of the patient's subjective sensation of smell. It had turned out in fact to have been an objective sensation originally, and one which was intimately associated with an experience – a little scene – in which opposing affects had been in conflict with each other: her regret at leaving the children and the slights which were nevertheless urging her to make up her mind to do so... The conflict between her affects had elevated the moment of the letter's arrival into a trauma, and the sensation of smell that was associated with this trauma persisted as its symbol.

Sigmund Freud, The case of Miss Lucy R., age 30, 1895

I had no problems when it was cold and there was a strong wind off the sea. But in April, when it started to be hot and it was dead calm, there was a stench of shit, and the gnats and mosquitoes moved in. It was unbearable... The roof turned into a stinking place, with gnats biting by day and mosquitoes by night. It was impossible to sleep.

In general, I'm not a lover of good smells. Right now I can't even remember any particular woman's perfume. I don't like smells like that. Either that or they don't interest me. On the other hand, I'll never forget the smell of the fresh shit of a boy attacked by sharks in the Gulf of Mexico. He was a tuna fisherman. He was going about his business in the stern of the boat, pulling up the splendid silver fish one by one, when he fell overboard. Three enormous sharks were swimming with the tunas, and in two bites they shredded his guts and ripped off his leg. We hauled him up very quickly, still living, his eyes wide with horror; everything happened in less than a minute. And he died immediately, bled to death, without ever being able to speak or understand what had happened to him. For months we were together in that stern, but I can't remember his face or his name. All I can remember clearly is the terrible stink of the boy, with his abdomen slashed open and his guts spilling excrement onto the boat's deck.

Pedro Juan Gutierrez,
Dirty Havana Trilogy, 2002

I know what burning smells like. I have not forgotten the death of my village, though it was a lifetime ago, for that too I caused. Smoke and scorch. Smoulder. Each thing that fire takes has a different odour. Bedclothes, bullock cart, cradle. That is how a village goes up in flame. A city would be different, buses and cars, sofa sets covered with vinyl, an exploding TV. But the smell of charred flesh is the same everywhere.

Chitra Banerjee Divakaruni,
The Mistress of Spices, 1997

LE FLACON

Il est de forts parfums pour qui toute matière
Est poreuse. On dirait qu'ils pénètrent le verre.
En ouvrant un coffret venu de l'Orient
Dont la serrure grince et rechigne en criant,

Ou dans une maison déserte quelque armoire
Pleine de l'âcre odeur des temps, poudreuse et noire,
Parfois on trouve un vieux flacon qui se souvient,
D'où jaillit toute vive une âme qui revient.

*[In the presence of some strong perfumes all matter is porous. They seem
to penetrate even glass. On opening a casket brought from the Orient whose
lock creaks and protests loudly,*
*Or, in a deserted house, some cupboard, full of the acrid smell of times
past, dusty and dark, sometimes we find an old scent bottle that remembers,
from which there springs, all alive, a returning soul.]*

Charles Baudelaire, Le Flacon, 1857

BUT I wasn't ready for the surprise the abandoned pipe had in
store for me. Hardly had I smoked the first puff than I forgot
the grand books I was going to write. Amazed and touched, I was
breathing the smells of the past winter which came back to me. I
had not touched my faithful friend since my return to France, and
London, the London I had experienced all myself in the past year,
came back to me. First the beloved fogs that wrap themselves
around one's brain and have a smell all of their own when they
penetrate through the window.

Stéphane Mallarmé, La Pipe, 1864

HE ceased to pace about the short space between the baptistery and the bath; he leaned against the window. His dizziness ended. He carefully stopped up the vials, and used the occasion to arrange his cosmetics. Since his arrival at Fontenay he had not touched them; and now was quite astonished to behold once more this collection formerly visited by so many women. The flasks and jars were lying heaped up against each other. Here, a porcelain box contained a marvellous white cream which, when applied on the cheeks, turns to a tender rose colour, under the action of the air – to such a true flesh-colour that it procures the very illusion of a skin touched with blood; there, lacquer objects incrusted with mother of pearl enclosed Japanese gold and Athenian green, the colour of the cantharis wing, gold and green which change to deep purple when wetted...

He handled this collection, formerly bought to please a mistress who swooned under the influence of certain aromatics and balms, – a nervous, unbalanced woman who loved to steep the nipples of her breasts in perfumes, but who never really experienced a delicious and overwhelming ecstasy save when her head was scraped with a comb or when she could inhale, amid caresses, the odour of perspiration, or the plaster of unfinished houses on rainy days, or of dust splashed by huge drops of rain during summer storms.

He mused over these memories, and one afternoon spent at Pantin through idleness and curiosity, in company with this woman at the home of one of her sisters, returned to him, stirring in him a forgotten world of old ideas and perfumes; while the two women prattled and displayed their gowns, he had drawn near the window and had seen, through the dusty panes, the muddy street sprawling before him, and had heard the repeated sounds of galoshes over the puddles of the pavement. This scene, already far removed, came to him suddenly, strangely and vividly.

Joris-Karl Huysmans,
Against the Grain, 1884

IT was almost dark in the room, and very hot, while the air was heavy with the mingled scent of mint, eau-de-cologne, camomile, and Hoffman's pastilles. The latter ingredient caught my attention so strongly that even now I can never hear of it, or even think of it, without my memory carrying me back to that dark, close room, and all the details of that dreadful time.

Leo Tolstoy, Childhood, 1852

FRANÇOISE would come in to light the fire, and in order to make it draw, would throw upon it a handful of twigs, the scent of which, forgotten for a year past, traced round the fireplace a magic circle within which, glimpsing myself poring over a book... I was as joyful, while remaining in my bedroom in Paris, as if I had been on the point of setting out for a walk along the Méséglise way...The scent, in the frosty air, of the twigs of brushwood was like a fragment of the past, an invisible ice-floe detached from some bygone winter advancing into my room, often, moreover, striated with this or that perfume or gleam of light, as though with different years in which I found myself once more submerged, overwhelmed, even before I had identified them, by the exhilaration of hopes long since abandoned.

Marcel Proust, The Captive, 1923

THERE are smells that define a home. Ours smelled of boiled gammon, parsley sauce and what Joan, in a futile attempt to be middle class, called "creamed" potatoes.

A smell which, encountered at another time, another place, would bring back every swirl of sitting-room carpet, every piece of knotty-pine kitchen unit, ach and every melamine cup and saucer; the creak of the green Parker-Knoll rocking-chair and the click of Joan's knitting needles... the scent of Dad's red and salmon begonias in the greenhouse; the smell of my Matey bubblebath, her Camay soap and his Signal toothpaste.

Nigel Slater, Toast, 2003

So, seeing the convolvulus in flower, she says to me: "Smell them, they smell of good honey; and do not forget them!" This is therefore the first revelation of the sense of smell that I remember; and by a link between memories and sensations that everyone knows, and cannot explain, I never smell convolvulus flowers without seeing the place in the Spanish mountains and the wayside where I first plucked them.

George Sand, Story of my Life, 1854-1855

The sense of smell is of the highest importance to the greater number of mammals – to some, as the ruminants, in warning them of danger; to others, as the Carnivora, in finding their prey; to others, again, as the wild boar, for both purposes combined. But the sense of smell is of extremely slight service, if any, even to the dark coloured races of men, in whom it is much more highly developed than in the white and civilised races. Nevertheless it does not warn them of danger, nor guide them to their food; nor does it prevent the Esquimaux from sleeping in the most fetid atmosphere, nor many savages from eating half-putrid meat. In Europeans the power differs greatly in different individuals, as I am assured by an eminent naturalist who possesses this sense highly developed, and who has attended to the subject. Those who believe in the principle of gradual evolution, will not readily admit that the sense of smell in its present state was originally acquired by man, as he now exists. He inherits the power in an enfeebled and so far rudimentary condition, from some early progenitor, to whom it was highly serviceable, and by whom it was continually used. In those animals which have this sense highly developed, such as dogs and horses, the recollection of persons and of places is strongly associated with their odour; and we can thus perhaps understand how it is, as Dr. Maudsley has truly remarked, that the sense of smell in man "is singularly effective in recalling vividly the ideas and images of forgotten scenes and places."

Charles Darwin, The Descent of Man, 1871

THE room is full of you! – As I came in
   And closed the door behind me, all at once
A something in the air, intangible,
Yet stiff with meaning, struck my senses sick! –
Sharp, unfamiliar odors have destroyed
Each other room's dear personality.
The heavy scent of damp, funereal flowers, –
The very essence, hush-distilled, of Death –
Has strangled that habitual breath of home
Whose expiration leaves all houses dead;
And wheresoe'er I look is hideous change.
Save here. Here 'twas as if a weed-choked gate
Had opened at my touch, and I had stepped
Into some long-forgot, enchanted, strange,
Sweet garden of a thousand years ago
And suddenly thought, "I have been here before!"
You are not here. I know that you are gone,
And will not ever enter here again.
And yet it seems to me, if I should speak,
Your silent step must wake across the hall;
If I should turn my head, that your sweet eyes
Would kiss me from the door. ...
And here are the last words your fingers wrote,
Scrawled in broad characters across a page
In this brown book I gave you....
...since you could not know, and it befell
That these are the last words your fingers wrote,
There is a dignity some might not see
In this, "I picked the first sweet-pea to-day."
To-day! Was there an opening bud beside it
You left until to-morrow? – O my love,
The things that withered, – and you came not back!
That day you filled this circle of my arms
That now is empty. (O my empty life!)
That day – that day you picked the first sweet-pea, –

And brought it in to show me! I recall
With terrible distinctness how the smell
Of your cool gardens drifted in with you.

Edna St Vincent Millay, Interim, 1917

NOTHING is more memorable than a smell. One scent can be unexpected, momentary, and fleeting, yet conjure up a childhood summer beside a lake in the Poconos, when wild blueberry bushes teemed with succulent fruit and the opposite sex was as mysterious as space travel; another, hours of passion on a moonlit beach in Florida, while the night-blooming cereus drenched the air with thick curds of perfume and huge sphinx moths visited the cereus in a loud purr of wings; a third, a family dinner of pot roast, noodle pudding, and sweet potatoes, during a myrtle-mad August in a Midwestern town, when both of one's parents were alive. Smells detonate softly in our memory like poignant land mines, hidden under the weedy mass of many years and experiences. Hit a tripwire of smell, and memories explode all at once. A complex vision leaps out of the undergrowth

Diane Ackerman,
A Natural History of the Senses, 1990

SMELL is a potent wizard that transports us across a thousand miles and all the years we have lived. The odor of fruits wafts me to my Southern home, to my childish frolics in the peach orchard. Other odors, instantaneous and fleeting, cause my heart to dilate joyously or contract with remembered grief. Even as I think of smells, my nose is full of scents that start awake sweet memories of summers gone and ripening grain fields far away.

The faintest whiff from a meadow where the new-mown hay lies in the hot sun displaces the here and the now. I am back again in the old red barn. My little friends and I are playing in the haymow. A huge mow it is, packed with crisp, sweet hay, from the top of which the smallest child can reach the straining rafters. In their stalls beneath are the farm animals.

Helen Keller, Sense and Sensibility, 1907

WHEN from a long-distant past nothing subsists, after the people are dead, after the things are broken and scattered, taste and smell alone, more fragile but more enduring, more immaterial, more persistent, more faithful, remain poised a long time, like souls, remembering, waiting, hoping, amid the ruins of all the rest; and bear unflinchingly, in the tiny and almost impalpable drop of their essence, the vast structure of recollection.

Marcel Proust, Swann's Way, 1913

INDEX

REFERENCES AND
COPYRIGHT NOTICES

While every effort has been made to secure permission to use the extracts in this collection, the editors may not always have been successful in tracking copyright. We apologise for any omission; notification of such should be addressed to the publisher.

Ackerman, Diane, A Natural History of the Senses, copyright © 1990 by Diane Ackerman. Used by permission of Random House, Inc.

Artaud , Pursuit of Fecality. From Selected Writings © 1988 The Regents of the University of California, University of California Press

Asselin, Giles, Ruth Mastron, Au Contraire: Figuring Out the French, © 2000 by Giles Asselin and Ruth Mastron, Intercultural Press

Atwood, Margaret, Cat's Eye. Copyright © 1988 by Margaret Atwood. Used by permission of Curtis Brown Group Ltd., London on behalf of Margaret Atwood

Auden, W.H., September 1939, reprinted by permission of Faber & Faber

Auden, W.H., The Poet and the City, reprinted by permission of Faber & Faber

Burgess, Thornton, The Adventures of Jimmy Skunk. Reprinted by permission of Dover Publications Ltd.

Burr, Chandler, The Emperor of Scent, published by William Heinemann Ltd. Reprinted by permission of The Random House Group Ltd

Burroughs, William, Naked Lunch. Reprinted by permission of Harper Collins UK, 2005

Calvino, Italo, The Name, The Nose, from Under the Jaguar Sun, Jonathan Cape, 1992. By permission of The Wylie Agency.

Carpenter, Edmund Snow, Eskimo Realities, Holt, Reinhart and Winston, 1973

Carter, Angela, The Fall River Axe Murders (from Saints and Strangers), Viking, 1986

Classen, Constance, Worlds of Sense: Exploring the Senses in History and Across Cultures, Routledge 1993

Colette, 'The South of France' in Earthly Paradise, published by Secker and Warburg. Reprinted by permission of The Random House Group Ltd.

Corbin, Alain, The Foul and the Fragrant, Harvard University Press, 1986

Courtemanche, Gil, A Sunday at the Pool in Kigali, Canongate, 2003

Cummings, E. E., here's to opening and up-ward, ireprinted from COMPLETE POEMS 1904-1962, by E.E. Cummings, edited by George J. Firmage, by permission of W.W. Norton & Company. Copyright © 1991 by the Trustees for the E.E. Cummings Trust and George James Firmage

Cummings, E. E., when my love comes to see me it's, reprinted from COMPLETE POEMS 1904-1962, by E.E. Cummings, edited by George J. Firmage, by permission of W.W. Norton & Company © 1991 by the Trustees for the E.E. Cummings Trust and George James Firmage

Cummings, E. E., and this day it was Spring.... us, reprinted from COMPLETE POEMS 1904-1962, by E.E. Cummings, edited by George J. Firmage, by permission of W.W. Norton & Company. Copyright © 1991 by the Trustees for the E.E. Cummings Trust and George James Firmage.

Dahl, Roald, Jack and the Beanstalk. From Revolting Rhymes, Jonathan Cape Ltd & Penguin Books. Reprinted with permission.

Dalrymple, William, City of Djinns. © William Dalrymple. Reprinted by permission of HarperCollins Publishers Ltd.

Desai, Anita, Fasting and Feasting, Chatto and Windus, 1999

Diner, Hasia R., Lower East Side Memories: A Jewish Place in America. Copyright © 2000 by Hasia R. Diner. Reprinted by permission of Princeton University Press

Divakaruni, Chitra Banerjee, Mistress of Spice. Reprinted by permission of The Random House Group Ltd.

Dupont, Florence, Daily Life in Ancient Rome. Reprinted by permissin of Blackwell Publishing.

Eliot, TS, from Preludes. Reprinted by permission of Faber & Faber

Eliot, TS, from Intro to A Choice of Kipling's Verse (in collected essays). Reprinted by permission of Faber & Faber

Eliot, TS, from A Dedication to My Wife. Reprinted by permission of Faber & Faber

Freud, Sigmund, Case of Lucy R, Sigmund Freud © Copyrights, The Institute of Psycho-Analysis and The Hogarth Press for permission to quote from THE STANDARD EDITION OF THE COMPLETE PSYCHOLOGICAL WORKS OF SIGMUND FREUD translated and edited by James Strachey. Reprinted by permission of The Random House Group Ltd.

Freud, Sigmund, Fixations of Preliminary Sexual Aims Sigmund Freud © Copyrights, The Institute of Psycho-Analysis and The Hogarth Press for permission to quote from THE STANDARD EDITION OF THE COMPLETE PSYCHOLOGICAL WORKS OF SIGMUND FREUD translated and edited by James Strachey. Reprinted by permission of The Random House Group Ltd.

Glover, Jon, Taxi. Reprinted by permission of Carcanet Press Ltd

Gutierrez, Pedro Juan, Dirty Havana Trilogy. Reprinted by permission of Faber & Faber

Helfgott Hyett, Barbara, 'The ovens' and excerpts from 'And I went in' and 'We walked into' from IN EVIDENCE: POEMS OF THE LIBERATION OF THE NAZI CONCENTRATION CAMPS © 1986. Reprinted by permission of the University of Pittsburgh Press.

Hemingway, Ernest, For Whom the Bell Tolls, published by Jonathan Cape. Reprinted by permission of The Random House Group Ltd.

Doolittle, Hilda, At Baia, from COLLECTED POEMS, 1912-1944, copyright © 1982 by The Estate of Hilda Doolittle. Reprinted by permission of New Directions Publishing Corp.

Jarrar, Nada Awar, Somewhere, Home. Copyright © 2003 by Nada Awar Jarrar. Reprinted by permission of HarperCollins Publishers Ltd.

Jellinek, Paul, The Psychological Basis of Perfumery, Blackie Academic and Professional, 1997

Kinder, Marsha, Kid's Media Culture, Duke University Press, 1999

Koeppen, Wolfgang, Death in Rome, Weidenfeld & Nicholson, 1956

Le Guérer, Annick, Scent, the mysterious and essential powers of smell, 1992. Reprinted by permission of The Random House Group Ltd.

Lux, Thomas After a Few Whiffs of Another World, from NEW & SELECTED POEMS, 1975-1995. Copyright © 1997 by Thomas Lux. Reprinted by permission of Houghton Mifflin Company

Mailer, Norman, Advertisements for Myself on the Way Out, Putnam's, 1959. By permission of The Wylie Agency.

Mayes, Francis, Under the Tuscan Sun. Published by Bantam Books. Reprinted by permission of The Random House Group Ltd.

Maugham, W.S., On a Chinese Screen. Published by William Heinemann. Reprinted by permission of The Random House Group Ltd.

Madsen, Axel, Coco Chanel, Bloomsbury, 1990

Mehta, Suketu, Maximum City, Headline Review, 2004

O'Rourke, P.J., Holidays in Hell, Picador, 2002

Orwell, George, Bookshop Memories. Reprinted by permission of Bill Hamilton as